FRANCIS: A SAINT WE SHARE

FRANCIS:
A Saint We Share

A Discussion Guide
for
Lutherans and Roman Catholics

GAIL RAMSHAW SCHMIDT

Paulist Press *New York/Ramsey*

Cover designed by Morris Berman
Cover art by Dennis Morinelli, S.A.

Library of Congress
Catalog Card Number: 82-60848

ISBN: 0-8091-2496-3

Published by Paulist Press
545 Island Road, Ramsey, N.J. 07446

Printed and bound in the
United States of America

Contents

Foreword vii

Introduction 1

1 His Ladylove 5

2 His Call 20

3 His Work 34

4 His Friends 47

5 His Befriending 61

6 His Sign 74

Notes 87

Program Suggestions 89

Foreword

A new chapter in the long story of relationships between Roman Catholics and Lutherans began in 1980. The 450th anniversary of the Augsburg Confession of 1530 became the occasion for hundreds of local dialogues and other gatherings of members from the two communions. Theologians of the two traditions had been talking seriously to each other, both on the national and international levels, since the time of the Second Vatican Council in the mid-1960s. Now the interest began to spread to many rank-and-file clergy and laity.

Many of the local dialogues found a helpful resource in *Exploring The Faith We Share: A Study Guide for Lutherans and Roman Catholics*, edited by the undersigned, and published by Paulist Press. This popular book continues to be useful for such groups, as well as for individuals and for couples in "mixed marriages." *Francis: A Saint We Share* is a sequel. It can be used by interconfessional groups who want to push further in dialogue; it can be used equally well by those who want to "explore the faith we share" for the first time.

This new study guide responds to the call by a committee of Lutheran and Roman Catholic bishops, at an October 1981 meeting, who asked parish and regional groups to join in celebrating the 800th anniversary of the birth of St. Francis of Assisi, and to study his life and ministry in light of the mission of the Church in our world. The bishops expressed concern that what was gained in ecumenical progress during the Augsburg Confession observances not fall into neglect. The staffs of the Graymoor Ecumenical Institute and of Lutheran Forum share that concern, and so we commissioned this book as we did the earlier one. We commend it to our sisters and brothers in both communions who would seriously explore what we hold in common and where we may differ in our Christian lives as an expression of our Christian faith.

Our hearty thanks to Gail Ramshaw Schmidt for dedication and imagination in the service of our shared heritage, and to Paulist Press for continuing commitment to the ministry of ecumenical communication.

Charles V. La Fontaine, S.A.
Editor, *Ecumenical Trends*
  and
Co-Director,
Graymoor Ecumenical
  Institute

Glenn C. Stone
Editor, *Lutheran Forum*
  and
Executive Director,
American Lutheran
  Publicity Bureau

May 31, 1982
Feast of the Visitation

Introduction

Many Christians now yearn for reconciliation within the Church of God. Often, when groups of us meet for dialogue, we discuss doctrine. Roman Catholics and Lutherans, beginning in 1980 with the Year of the Augsburg Confession, have been meeting to compare and contrast their understanding of baptism, the Eucharist, ministry, and the Church. And so it should be. We must explain ourselves so that we can discover where we agree and seek to understand where we differ.

Doctrinal discussions are not the *only* means of exploring the faith we share. Increasingly, Christians enjoy a common liturgy, and many find that in their shared symbols, texts, hymns, and patterns of worship there is already recognized and celebrated a unity which is greater than our denominational interpretations of that liturgy. Another way we share the faith is our ecumenical efforts to serve the world. Here, we are given the charge to work alongside one another and thus in Christian love demonstrate the faith we share.

This study guide offers yet another way to explore the faith we share. The Church has been formed by grace through history. God's saving of the world continues through time, beyond the New Testament period. It is bound up with the lives of the baptized people who with their actions shaped the Church and altered human history in their praise of God. The history of the Church's people is our common history. It is an important part of the Christian life we already share. For the most part, it is one single history. While we cannot ignore the divergence in Roman Catholic and Lutheran history during the last 450 years, we must explore together our common 1,500 years of shared history in order better to understand ourselves and one another.

The year 1982 is being observed throughout the Christian Church as the eight hundredth birthday of Francis of Assisi. The "little poor man" is a believer whose sanctity most Christians in succeeding generations have accepted as exemplary. In fact, he has been acclaimed the patron of all sorts of worthy causes by Christians of every type and every age. He has been one of the most popular Christian figures for many Protestants and is one of the Church's holy people whom the secular world also recognizes and acclaims. Kurt Waldheim, former Secretary-General of the United Nations, has spoken of Francis as an inspiration for world peace. Even the United States Postal Service is honoring Francis by issuing a commemorative stamp. Surely we must get to know this great man better. Lutheran and Roman Catholic bishops in the United States have urged their people to join in a serious study of this remarkable saint. So we do just that, hoping that our shared study will become a goad to our Christian life and an inspiration for our Christian imagination.

What have we of Francis to study? He left no autobiography, only some prayers, several letters, and the Rules for the Franciscan Order. We do not know his birthdate; we are not even sure of his birth year; there are many gaps in our knowledge about his time. What we have are early biographies: Franciscans Thomas of Celano and Bonaventure wrote the most extended ones, and there are half a dozen other early writings which tell the famous stories. Thus, what we have are the early interpretations of Francis, the Franciscan movement's response to the life of the troubadour from Assisi through whom they shared the life of Christ.

We say we share the Christian life. Both Roman Catholics and Lutherans share in the same baptism and Eucharist from which Francis received his life in Christ. In this basic way we share the same Christian life Francis lived. Of course, he was no twentieth-century Christian, Lutheran or Roman Catholic. His radical response to the cross of Christ may seem quite foreign to our sensibilities and our patterns of piety. Perhaps we will find ourselves closer to one another than either of us is to Francis. He embraced Lady Poverty—not a popular ladylove (Chapter I). His call (Chapter II) came from the open Bible. He worked (Chapter III) in literal and spiritual ways to repair the Church of Christ. He named everyone, even wild animals, his friends (Chapter IV). Those who would be his enemies he befriended (Chapter V). His sign (Chapter VI) is ours—the cross. He lived and died in the shadow of that sign as we are called to do.

This study brings us together for six sessions. Each chapter begins with a quotation from one of the early biographies of Francis. Thus, we encounter some of the most famous stories from his life. Following each narrative is a discussion in which we compare and contrast Francis' life and faith with our own. Written into this section are a number of potential discussion questions. Do we agree or disagree with Francis? Why? Can Francis' stunning model of discipleship move us closer to the cross and, thus, closer to one another? Each chapter concludes with a prayer or plea which Francis himself wrote. Perhaps our joint meetings can begin or conclude in this way, as Francis would wish, in joint prayer to God. Thus we undertake this study in the hope that by sharing the life of Francis, we will share more fully both in one another's life and in the life of Christ.

We pray a prayer of Francis:

All-powerful, all holy, most high and supreme God, sovereign good, all good, every good, you who alone are good, it is to you we must give all praise, all glory, all thanks, all honor, all blessing; to you we must refer all good always. Amen.[1]

CHRONOLOGY

1181	(1182?) Summer or fall, Francis born in Assisi, baptized John, nicknamed Francis.
1199	Civil war between nobles and townspeople in Assisi.
1202	War between Assisi and Perugia: Francis, 20, prisoner for a year.
1204	Vision of Christ keeps Francis from going off to war.
1206	Francis, 24, wears hermit's habit and repairs churches.
1208	Francis, 26, becomes itinerant preacher. Bernard, Peter, Giles join him.
1209	Francis goes to Rome to seek approval of the Order.
1211	(1212?) Consecration of Clare.
1213	Biographer Thomas of Celano joins the Franciscan Order.
1215	Francis, 33, attends the Fourth Lateran Council in Rome, meets Dominic.
1216	Pope Honorius grants the Portiuncola Pardon.
1219	Francis, 37, preaches to the Sultan.
1220	Francis resigns as leader of the Order.
1221	Francis writes the first Rule. Pope approves the Third Order. The Chapter of Mats is held, and 5,000 friars attend.
1223	Francis' second Rule is approved by the Pope. The Christmas crèche Mass.
1224	September 17: Francis receives the stigmata.
1225	In extreme physical pain Francis writes the Canticle.
1226	October 3. Francis, 44, dies at Portiuncola, is buried October 4.
1228	Pope Gregory IX canonizes Francis.

1
His Ladylove

Soon after Francis had returned to Assisi, his companions elected him king of the revels, and gave him a free hand to spend what he liked in the preparation of a sumptuous banquet as he had often done on other occasions. After the feast they left the house and started off singing through the streets. Francis' companions were leading the way, and he, holding his wand of office, followed them at a distance. Instead of singing, he was listening very attentively. All of a sudden the Lord touched his heart, filling it with such surpassing sweetness that he could neither speak nor move. He could only feel and hear this overwhelming sweetness which detached him so completely from all other physical sensations that, as he said later, had he been cut to pieces on the spot he could not have moved.

When his companions looked around, they saw him in the distance and turned back. To their amazement they saw that he was transformed into another man, and they asked him, "What were you thinking of? Why didn't you follow us? Were you thinking of getting married?"

Francis answered in a clear voice: "You are right: I was thinking of wooing the noblest, richest, and most beautiful bride ever seen." His friends laughed at him, saying he was a fool and did not know what he was saying; in reality he had spoken by a divine revelation. The bride was none other than that form of true religion which he embraced, and which, above any other, is noble, rich, and beautiful in its poverty. From that hour he began to consider himself as naught and to despise all those things he had formerly cherished; but he still did so imperfectly, not being as yet entirely detached from worldly vanities. He gradually withdrew from the tumult of earthly things and applied himself secretly to receive Jesus Christ into his soul with that pearl of great price which he so desired as to be willing to sell all he possessed in order to gain it. . . . He was already a benefactor of the poor, but from this time onward he resolved never to refuse alms to anyone who begged in God's name, but rather to give more willingly and abundantly than ever before. If a poor person begged of him when he was far from home, he would always give him money, if possible; when he had none he would give his belt or buckle; or, if he had not even these, he would find a hiding place and, taking off his shirt, give it to the beggar for the love of God.

Legend of the Three Companions
(ca. 1325)[1a]

KNIGHT OF POVERTY

King of the revels, Francis was called. As a young man he was famous in Assisi because he was the life of the party. It was Francis who sang the troubadour's songs, who improvised romantic ballads, and who wore the finest fashions. It was Francis who paid the bills for the banquets, for as the son of one of Assisi's most successful merchants, he had money to spend on frivolities. His easy ways and charming manners helped him become one of the most popular socialites in town. The old stories tell how he entertained his friends by singing the love songs of courtly adventures. His imagination was filled with the tales of knights and ladies, of noble battles and terrifying missions, of rescuing a maiden and wooing a loved one, all for the glory of God and to the honor of the lady. To display your lady's token as you rode off to vanquish the enemy—such was the dream of young Francis, king of the revels.

The world in which Francis sang of knights and ladies was one of enormous social upheaval. The old feudal system, in which the lords owned the land and granted protection to the poor, while claiming most of their produce, was falling apart. Serfs no longer paid their traditional tolls and fees. Those who were able escaped to the cities to work freely for wages. Lords were land-poor, and they banded together to try to reclaim prerogatives which were already forgotten. Benedictine monasteries were among the wealthy landowners struggling in a new world in which the urbanized merchant and the city's mayor had new and disruptive power. The emperor allied with landowners to protect the earlier values, and the various levels of churchly authority—local parishes, bishops, abbots, the Pope—entered the fracas to claim a piece of a pie cut in new ways. Cities were destroyed by civil war. Perhaps the major symbol of this emerging age was money—money which created a middle class, bought new loyalties, dethroned land, and enriched the Church's treasuries.

The stories tell us that in his early twenties Francis began a new life. He had recovered somewhat, although never fully, from the severe illness he contracted while, after fighting in a war between two cities, and being captured, he was imprisoned for a year in wretched circumstances. He recovered, again the king of the revels, learning the trade of the rich cloth merchant. But then he began to see visions. He had several overwhelming religious experiences: a voice spoke to him on a roadway; a crucifix challenged him to new directions; the Gospel lessons seemed to be aimed directly at him.

At the beginning of this chapter, we read about one such experience, after which Francis embraced poverty. In the language of the troubadour, the young poet and adventurer chose his love, Lady Poverty. Bonaventure later called Francis "the valiant knight of Christ" and wrote: "He had chosen the privilege of Poverty for his special boast, calling it his mother, his bride, and his lady fair."[2] Francis' tone remained the same. He was the knight living for his lady, he was the lover, he abandoned all to serve the fair one. But the subject of the song, the object of his affections, was radically altered, from some respectable middle-class young woman or the daughter of a financially depressed landowner to the ragged woman Poverty, now made lovely by the love of the knight.

The stories tell more. When inspired to donate money to rebuild a church, he took expensive cloth from his father's stock and sold it for the necessary cash. When his father hauled him before the bishop for retribution, Francis stripped himself naked before the assembly. By letting go of his fine clothes, he made himself a symbol of the poverty he had embraced. He donned a poor man's garb of sackcloth, and when it was torn, he mended it with yet another ragged piece of sackcloth.

Francis retained his radical rejection of the mercantile world even when his Order had grown to hundreds of followers. The first written Rule of the Order, 1221, reads, "I strictly forbid all the friars to accept money in any form, either personally or through an intermediary. . . . As wages for their labor they may accept anything necessary for their temporal needs, for themselves or their brethren, except money in any form."[3] The scholars debate how much Francis agreed to the softening of this original vow as the Order grew in size, but no one doubts that his intent was the total commitment of the knight to his lady and the joyful embrace of Lady Poverty. Francis requested that after he died he be placed naked on the ground for the time it takes to walk a mile, in a final acceptance of the nothingness which was his human life. Shortly after Francis' death, an imaginative narrative of the conversation between Francis and his lady became popular among Franciscans. Even in the title we see the troubadour's imagery married to the Christian faith: "The Sacred Romance of Saint Francis with Lady Poverty."

POVERTY IN AN AFFLUENT CULTURE

A great distance lies between this troubadour of God, this lover of Lady Poverty, and us. Even those few among us who have chosen the ideals of poverty are required, in this world where money has conquered land and castle, to use cash. Those among us who are by circumstance poor hardly embrace it as a joyful choice for life. It is here, then, in this radical marriage of Francis with Lady Poverty, that we begin our conversation. How do our various traditions respond to the call of Lady Poverty? If we do not embrace her, what does the command of Jesus mean, "Sell all you have and give to the poor"? How do Christians, no matter which denomination or tradition, live within capitalism? How do we live within a culture which ridicules the sackcloth of the friar? This topic, the first one offered us by the young convert Francis, is one in which our responses may fall into lines other than denominational ones. Yet we begin in the hope that in our mutual sharing of the life of Francis we may enlighten ourselves and one another in the ongoing conversation within the one Church.

The voice of the ascetic has always been heard in the Church. Paul advised a restrained life-style in light of the rapid approach of the new age. The Egyptian desert fathers went into the wilderness, turning toward emptiness in order to be ready for the kingdom. The Church recalls the life of many who lived with minimal comforts in order to share their goods with others. Radical ascetics gave up all and became dependent on others for subsistence in order to demonstrate their dependency on God. Mystics lived the life of poverty in order that their minds could be better focused on the richness of God.

The Church has always seen in the life of the poor a sign of God's grace. The "poor of God" is an Hebraic expression for those whom God will save. In our singing of Mary's "Magnificat" (Luke 1), we mean to join with the lowly and the hungry to receive the Gospel. In the second Christian millennium there arose entire orders, communities of women and men who sought to live the life of poverty. Even though the Order held property, the individuals did not, for they vowed personal poverty and adopted communal minimalism. Roman Catholic orders today struggle with the meaning of the vow of poverty in a world in which so much of human interaction is monetary. The famed gesture of Pope John XXIII washing the feet of Rome's slum beggars reminded us again of the Church's ideal of poverty. The entire world joins in amazement at Mother Teresa of Calcutta who has dedicated herself to a life of poverty and service to the poor.

Certain Protestants have also been attracted to the ideal of poverty. Small Protestant communities sprang up aspiring to live a New Testament life of individual poverty. The Hutterites have been one of the longest surviving of such groups. Utopian communities which once settled in America cherished the Christian ideal of communal property. Alive and well among us are Mennonites with their pledge for simple living. There are also small Protestant monasteries and convents. The extraordinary Taizé community in France, for example, holds goods in common and annually empties its bank accounts of any profits.

But in general the Protestant pattern has been different from the Roman Catholic one. Most small utopian communities either died out or became financially prosperous. Furthermore, Lutheranism often tended to appeal to the urban middle class and to successful farmers who survived hardships and with frugality rose up out of a life of the most desperate poverty. Lutherans retained a memory of the ideal of poverty, at least until recently, when the clergy, the deaconess, and the parochial school teacher, as models of the exemplary Christian, were at best underpaid and yet were leaders in financial tithing. Tithing as we know it is largely a product of American Protestantism. It is one vehicle through which a middle-class religious tradition has kept alive Francis' vision of the relative value of money.

So, who are we? Some of us have vowed poverty; others are investment counselors. Many of us are cutting back on extras because of inflation, but few, if any, who read these words are genuinely hungry. We live to a great degree within the world which Francis saw coming to birth—the world of money, and not only of money, but the world of credit. It is said that the strongest argument for churches to start using credit cards for contributions is that the gifts will be bigger. We tend to carry not quite enough cash, and so we think bigger, financially, with a plastic card in our hands. Thus we live, not only on the money we have received from others, but even more on the money we will receive from others, the society held together by a great financial bond of money owed. Your employer owes you today's wage; your salary check has not yet come; your credit is overextended; you cannot pay at the grocery store until an assistance check arrives. We cooperate with capitalism, whether or not we believe in it. Capitalism encourages spending more money by describing that expenditure as essential to the continuing health of the country. If I cannot pay my entire credit card balance, I am rewarded by having my credit extended.

In such a world one sees terrifying cracks in the facade. The poor are with us. The unemployed know a kind of poverty which challenges the capitalist vision. Such poverty is the hag of terror, hardly the Lady of Francis' dreams. Furthermore, our own survival, if it shall be, is confronted by miserable starvation elsewhere in the world. The hunger of many calls to us across the checkout counter.

CHRISTIANS AND WORLD POVERTY

The first question which arises for twentieth-century Roman Catholics and Lutherans is the issue of world poverty. Francis wrote in his final testament, "When I was in sin, the sight of lepers nauseated me beyond measure; but then God himself led me into their company, and I had pity on them. When I had once become acquainted with them, what had previously nauseated me became a source of spiritual and physical consolation for me."[4] Surely, Francis' embrace of Lady Poverty calls us to embrace the poor of our world. They are not only the world's hungry—as if the starving peoples were not enough to care for! They are also the "lepers" whom Francis embraced: the social outcasts, refugees, the morally repulsive, the homeless. The list is endless—bag ladies, migrant workers, criminal ex-offenders, hordes crowded into shanties in concentration camps.

It was not because Lady Poverty was so ugly in her sores and rags that Francis pitied her. Rather, with a converted consciousness he saw her as the most beautiful, the most desired lover. What are the resources of our separate traditions and of our present structures which will assist us in such a conversion, such a turn toward the poor of the world in loving embrace? It is not enough that we applaud Mother Teresa's struggles, that the Poor Clares fast, that Lutheran synods collect money for world hunger. Our joint efforts to bring God's love to the world begin in our own conversion. In the example of Francis, that conversion is toward the poor. Jesus dined with prostitutes. Francis embraced the leper. We too must adopt the poor, the rejected.

Even our present political tendency to close government coffers requires that the third sector—the already non-profit part of society—take up more of the feeding and clothing of the world, both in our own land and abroad. The community's needs are not too lowly a place to begin our embrace of the poor. Early in his twenties, when Francis was still seeking a knightly vocation, he left home on horseback to join a noble army which would vindicate truth. On his way, in radiant garb of a conquering hero, on a fine steed, he had a vision of Jesus questioning his motives and saying, "Go back to the place of your birth, for through me your vision will have a spiritual fulfillment."[5] Perhaps, as we commemorate Francis, our crusading should begin at home. Perhaps together we should embrace the local leper and in such an embrace find ourselves drawn closer to one another.

THE ASCETIC IDEAL

Of course Francis embraced not only the poor, but *poverty itself*. Thus, we face a second question—the choice of a life of poverty. Choosing poverty is not a socially acceptable activity these days. Roman Catholics maintain a tradition in which poverty is one avenue of religious devotion. In many Lutheran circles, the experience of the European Enlightenment and of immigration to North America has made a choice for poverty not only abhorrent but unfathomable. For many contemporary Lutherans and Roman Catholics, personal asceticism is not an item on the agenda. Few of us give up anything for Lent, although occasionally one hears of an overweight Christian who uses the Lenten fast to lose some pounds. We smile, slowly, sadly, at such a diminution of the ascetic ideal. How do we well-fed folks answer the call to sell all we have and give to the poor?

There is a powerful cultural antidote to asceticism and all its weaker cousins in the popular contemporary "human potential movement." We see its evidence on book jackets throughout the land. The movement, at its worst, sees human salvation as possible through the power of the self to take charge. It urges us to attend first to self as the primary human focus, as logically prior to any creative possibilities we may have outside the self and in the world. The human potential movement offers a challenge to Christianity today. What is the focus of the human being? We live only once! I'm OK! I'm Number One! Surrounded by such ideas, we sense that the ideal of the ascetic, for whom the body and the self are a sacrifice to God and a vehicle for service to others, is both strange and ill-fitting. How well does the sackcloth of Francis hang in the same closet as designer jeans? Paradoxically, incongruously, at least.

CHALLENGE OF HUMILITY

Physical poverty is only a part of Francis' commitment to his Lady. In his humility of spirit, we are given a third challenge. Spiritual humility is an ideal perhaps as difficult to attain as physical poverty. The stories tell that when Francis found himself thinking better of himself than of others, he stripped himself naked and preached in the town square, thus receiving all the ridicule due such behavior. Not only his body but also his spirit was nothingness before God. His spirit was humble. In modern English, the word "humility" has overtones of humiliation. Thus we cannot think of humility without questioning the appropriateness of such a virtue. Where in the contemporary Church have we such examples of spiritual humility? How can we rethink authority in the Church in order that the leader may be the one who serves? When Francis organized his followers into a religious community, he requested that they be called the "Little Brothers," the Friars Minor, and that no father figure, no abbot, rule over them. No lords among us, and no lords to the rest of the world, Francis suggests.

Lutheranism has its own treatise on humility—Martin Luther's commentary on the "Magnificat." Luther lauds and emulates Mary for her total humility, her poverty of spirit, her faith in God. "When the holy virgin experienced what great things God was working in her despite her insignificance, her lowliness, poverty, and inferiority, the Holy Spirit taught her this deep insight and wisdom: that God is the kind of Lord who does nothing but exalt those of low degree and put down the mighty from their thrones."[6] Luther's praise is grounded in Mary's humility, "a simple maiden, tending the cattle and doing housework, and doubtless esteemed no more than any poor maidservant today."[7] This attitude is familiar to Lutherans: we are graced if we are humble because only within such humility can faith and obedience arise. The human is humble, yes, worthless, before God. "We are beggars, this is true," were among Luther's final words, spoken on his deathbed. The actions of Francis demonstrate this poverty dramatically. The "little poor one," as Francis has been called, donned rags and died naked for the love of God.

The Gospel call, to which these are different responses, is the same. The Gospel call, "Blessed are the poor in spirit, for theirs is the kingdom of heaven," speaks to the poor in spirit *now*, of a kingdom available *now*, in the time of the King which is *now*. The resurrection has already brought in the final age. "Herald of the Great King," Francis called himself. Only in the light of the new age already begun does the embrace of poverty and a life of humility make any sense. In this new age, we are joyful creatures before God. In the kingdom, we can rejoice even in our creatureliness. We can rest assured that a life of humility is blessed by the King of the new age as an appropriate lifestyle for the Christian faithful.

AN IMITATION OF CHRIST

We must still ask a fourth question. *Why* did Francis embrace Lady Poverty? Trained in psychology, we want to know why he made that decision. Was he rebelling against his commercially successful father? Was he rejecting an emerging social system grounded in money? Was he a courtly lover seeking a unique lady to serve? Was he, plain and simple, a fool?

Not much is extant of Francis' writings: half a dozen letters, the Rules, some prayers, a final testament. Not even the famous "St. Francis' Prayer" was actually written by him. In the few words we have, in his actions, in the Franciscan literature written after his death, we can discover his primary reason for embracing Lady Poverty. In the first Rule, he wrote: "The Rule and life of the Friars is to live in obedience, in chastity, and without property, following the teachings and the footsteps of our Lord Jesus Christ."[8] Likeness to Christ is the answer. Following Christ in all things is the consequence of conversion. Medieval Christians believed that Jesus was wretchedly poor. When Jesus began preaching, he abandoned whatever home he had—even Mary is portrayed as the poorest of the land—to wander with God, without a job, without a roof, wearing a cloak donated by attendant women. Jesus was so hungry that he had to pick grain off the stalk on the sabbath. He died among the outcast. He was laid in a borrowed tomb. He emptied himself, writes Paul. Francis saw in the poverty of Jesus an ideal, a way by which he could empty himself and thus be filled with God.

Here, as in the question of poverty, our traditions offer us different words and images. Growth in grace toward the likeness of Christ is language familiar to Roman Catholics. Because the medieval Church closely associated a likeness to Christ with monastic life and mystical experience, the Reformation Churches avoided that vocabulary and spoke more often about forgiveness from Christ. Yet Lutherans also have ways to articulate the response to God's call. Martin Luther spoke about our daily remembrance of baptism as conformity to Christ, a daily death to sin, a daily rising to new life. Dietrich Bonhoeffer, who died a martyr under the Nazis, reminds us how great is the cost of discipleship, how total that discipleship must be. To be like Christ, to imitate Christ, to follow Christ, to conform to Christ—it is through phrases like these that we approach the meaning of Francis' commitment to Lady Poverty.

Francis, king of revels, became Francis, "Il Poverello," the little poor one. Francis, winsome troubadour, became Francis, valiant knight of Christ. He married Lady Poverty, in wedding clothes of sackcloth, with the Eucharist and little else as wedding feast. He firmly resolved never to own a home. He gave away all his wedding gifts to the needy. He challenges us to feed the poor, to control our use of money, to practice asceticism, to embrace humility, to live freely in this new age, to become like Jesus Christ. Now, what shall we do with this Francis? Rather, what shall he do with us?

We proclaim Francis' Praises of the Virtues:[9]

> Hail, Queen Wisdom! The Lord save you,
>> with your sister, pure, holy Simplicity.
> Lady Holy Poverty, God Keep you,
>> with your sister, holy Humility.
> Lady Holy Love, God keep you,
>> with your sister, holy Obedience.

All holy virtues,
>God keep you,
>God, from whom you proceed and come.
In all the world there is not a man
>who can possess any one of you
>without first dying to himself.
The man who practices one and does not offend against
>the others
>>possesses all;
The man who offends against one,
>possesses none and violates all.
Each and every one of you
>puts vice and sin to shame.
Holy Wisdom puts Satan
>and all his wiles to shame.
Pure and holy Simplicity puts
>all the learning of this world,
>all natural wisdom, to shame.
Holy Poverty puts to shame
>all greed, avarice,
>and all the anxieties of this life.
Holy Humility puts pride to shame,
>and all the inhabitants of this world
>and all that is in the world.
Holy Love puts to shame all the temptations
>of the devil and the flesh
>and all natural fear.
Holy Obedience puts to shame
>all natural and selfish desires.
It mortifies our lower nature
>and makes it obey the spirit
>and our fellow men.
Obedience subjects a man
>to everyone on earth,

And not only to men,
>   but to all the beasts as well
>   and to the wild animals,
So that they can do what they like with him,
>   as far as God allows them.

2
His Call

But when on a certain day the Gospel was read in that church, how the Lord sent his disciples out to preach, the holy man of God, assisting there, understood somewhat the words of the Gospel; after Mass he humbly asked the priest to explain the Gospel to him more fully. When he had set forth for him in order all these things, the holy Francis, hearing that the disciples of Christ should not possess gold or silver or money, nor carry along the way script, or wallet, or bread, or a staff, that they should not have shoes, or two tunics, but that they should preach the kingdom of God and penance, immediately cried out exultingly: "This is what I wish, this is what I seek, this is what I long to do with all my heart." Then the holy father, overflowing with joy, hastened to fulfill that salutary word he had heard, and he did not suffer any delay to intervene before beginning devoutly to perform what he had heard. He immediately put off his shoes from his feet, put aside the staff from his hands, was content with one tunic, and exchanged his leather girdle for a small cord. He designed for himself a tunic that bore a likeness to the cross, that by means of it he might beat off all temptations of the devil; he designed a very rough tunic so that by it he might crucify the flesh with all its vices and sins; he designed a very poor and mean tunic, one that would not excite the covetousness of the world. The other things that he had heard, however, he longed with the greatest diligence and the greatest reverence to perform. For he was *not a deaf hearer of the Gospel, but committing all that he had read to praiseworthy memory, he tried diligently to carry it out to the letter.*

From then on he began to preach penance to all with great fervor of spirit and joy of mind, edifying his hearers with his simple words and his greatness of heart. His words were like a burning fire, penetrating the inmost reaches of the heart, and it filled the minds of all the hearers with admiration.

The First Life
(Thomas of Celano, 1229)[10]

HERALD OF THE GOSPEL

Francis' first biographer writes that during the several years of Francis' conversion his encounter with the Gospels was decisive. Francis went to church for the Eucharist. He was, in fact, "assisting," perhaps taking the liturgical role of deacon. The Gospel was read, in Latin, of course; the Bible was opened up for the assembly. This proclaimed Word, about which Francis inquired, inspired him to renew his life. There are many other such stories in which Francis heard the Gospel read, applied the words to himself, preached the open book to others, and commissioned his followers to do the same.

The radical call which we associate with Jesus' commission to the apostles became Francis' personal commission. What he heard proclaimed—sell all you have, take no money, deny yourself, follow me—he obeyed literally, as few Christians before or since have done. If Jesus commanded it, Francis followed it. His embrace of poverty, his choice of a poor worker's tunic, his refusal to use money—these decisions were not the result of some personal idiosyncrasy. Essentially, they were acts of obedience to the words of the open book.

In another famous story, Bernard, a neighbor from Assisi,

came to Francis for spiritual direction, only shortly after Francis' conversion. Francis' advice was this: he took Bernard into a church, found the Gospel book, and asked the priest to read at random three Gospels from the lectionary. "Just open the book," we can hear trusting Francis say. "God will speak in the open book." The three successive Gospels which Bernard heard advised him to sell what he has, to take nothing for the journey, and to deny himself. The open book won for Christ another radical follower of the Word. Bernard, once a noble, became Francis' first companion.

Although Francis was attracted to a life of contemplative prayer, he believed that his primary call was to preach the open book to the world. He preached penance—not the complicated late medieval system of ecclesiastical obligations which the Reformation Churches criticized, but biblical penance, a turning away from self to God in a spirit of repentance, a radical newness of life in the cross.

Francis preached this open Bible to everyone. The story says that when he preached a simple parabolic homily to Pope Innocent III, the Pope and his entire court were profoundly moved by his rendering of the Gospel. He preached in his town square to his family and friends, he preached to outcast lepers, he preached to his companions—always the open Gospel book. His famous sermons to the birds point more to his commitment to preaching than to his commitment to birds. In one of the more memorable homiletic illustrations of all time, Francis once entered the pulpit naked, and in a voice of utter simplicity began "to preach so marvelously about contempt for the world, holy penance, holy voluntary poverty, the desire for the kingdom of heaven, and about the nakedness and humiliations and most holy passion of our Lord Jesus Christ crucified that the whole crowd of men and women who had gathered for the sermon in great numbers began to weep very bitterly."[11] Inspired by the nakedness of Christ, Francis became naked and thus preached the Word of Christ.

Francis maintained that all he found necessary was a simple literal proclamation of the Gospel. In contrast with his contemporary, Dominic, Francis did not require rigorous biblical scholarship as a prerequisite for preaching. He did not feel that those companions of his who were illiterate would be hampered in their preaching, because the open book could be heard in the reading of the Gospel and then proclaimed again. He was deeply distressed when, arriving back home after a journey, he found that one Little Brother was holding a faculty position, teaching theology at a university. Francis' genius lay in the proclamation of the radical Gospel's call in simple, persuasive tone without recourse to scholarly apparatus. Anyone, he felt, could hear the Word and follow it.

CHRIST IN THE BIBLE

This is not to say that Francis was biblically simple-minded. One need only look at his "Office of the Passion" to realize his biblical knowledge and his interpretive skills. This Office is a compilation of biblical passages which the friars and nuns used in praying the Divine Office (morning prayer, evening prayer, and six other prayer services scattered every few hours throughout the day). The biblical passages which Francis prescribed demonstrate not only that he knew the psalms well, but also that he, like the ancient Church Fathers and like Martin Luther, saw Christ throughout the Bible. Contemporary Christians will remember that Dietrich Bonhoeffer saw in the psalms of lament the crucifixion of Christ, in the psalms of praise the victory of Christ, and in the communal psalms the body of Christ assembled.

Francis' writings are filled with biblical phrases. His prayers echo biblical language. Even his Rule for the Franciscan Order, especially the first version of 1221, contains one biblical passage after another. "The Rule and life of the friars is to live in obedience, in chastity, and without property, following the teaching and the footsteps of our Lord Jesus Christ who says, 'If thou wilt be perfect, go, sell what thou hast, and give to the poor, and thou shalt have treasure in heaven, and come, follow me.' "[12] This first paragraph of the Rule quotes three more Bible passages containing the call to radical discipleship. The Rule included more than eighty biblical quotations. By the very form and content of the Rule, Francis conveys his reliance on Scripture. The Gospels, the epistles, the prophets, and the psalms are most often Francis' companions, but books like Tobit and Acts are also quoted.

Because he insisted that the Word be preached, Francis and his companions began to commission missionaries early in their common life together. One of the decisions made by the Little Brothers at their first general chapter was to send groups of friars throughout Italy, France and Germany, the brothers going two by two in the name of the Lord. Francis' commission of the brothers, as might be expected, was shaped by biblical injunctions. The friars had a particularly wretched time in Germany. Because they could not speak the language, they were ridiculed and abused. Apparently they felt that their ignorance of the language was no great deterrent! Francis wanted to preach the Word in France, the land of his boyhood dreams, but a cardinal who wanted him for other service convinced him not to go on such a mission. Francis did most of his preaching nearer home.

Because Francis wanted the words of the open book to be proclaimed and received, he planned his famous Christmas service. To allow the Christmas Gospel to be heard in all its abject poverty and amazing grace, Francis decided to hold the Christmas Eve service out-of-doors, on a hillside, with a manger, the hay, the ox and the ass as the setting in which the Midnight Mass would be celebrated. Francis was deacon, and he took the part of the assisting minister. As was the custom, his role was to chant the Christmas Gospel. At that service this troubadour preached "charming words concerning the nativity of the poor King and the little town of Bethlehem. Frequently too, when he wished to call Christ Jesus, he would call him simply the Child of Bethlehem, aglow with overflowing love for him."[13] All the townspeople came with candles to worship, and it is said that at least one worshiper saw a vision of the Christ Child in that manger-made-eucharistic table. From Francis' determination to preach the Christmas Gospel, inspired by that spectacular midnight proclamation, came the Western tradition of displaying Christmas crèches in homes and town squares.

While we see one side of Francis in meeting his Lady Poverty, we view another aspect when we open the book. For him, the Bible was always open, speaking penance and grace, giving literal orders for the future, providing words with which to preach and to commission his companions. Not as a scholarly theologian, not as an ordained priest, but as a simple, faithful, itinerant preacher, Francis read the open book and obeyed.

CHURCHES OF THE WORD

The image of Francis preaching the open Bible is appealing, especially to Lutherans, because the Reformation Churches, and particularly Lutheranism, have been stereotyped as preachers. We should not forget that the Church has another Order of Preachers, the Dominicans. They find in Francis an inspiration for their vocation to preaching and call him one of their holy fathers. Of course, Lutherans do prize excellent preachers. Many Lutherans still call their clergy "preachers." For much of Lutheran history Sunday has been essentially a day for preaching. Lutheran seminarians study Greek and Hebrew, biblical exegesis and preaching as major constituents of their training. Many Lutheran confirmation classes require youth to take sermon notes. Lutherans broadcast sermons on radio and publish daily homilies as standard devotional guides. These practices are offspring of the Reformation emphasis on renewal in the Word. God comes to us in the Word. Thus, it must be proclaimed, received and believed.

Like Francis, Martin Luther is often pictured as a proclaimer of the Word, whether before ecclesiastical officials, in parish pulpits or at dinner table. In many statues he holds an open Bible. It is not an oversimplification to say that the Gospel as spoken Word was the basis for Luther's religious experience. Of course, by "Word" Luther meant more than a page of words, a text of a book. "Word" for him meant Christ, Christ alive, Christ in the sacrament, Christ in the proclamation. Like Francis, Luther did not read the Bible for its scholarly or historical interest. Unlike Francis, he was a trained biblical scholar, theologian, and linguist. For Luther as for Francis, the proclamation of the Word was meant to be for life, for turning from self, for living for God. Lutheranism has always wanted to preach the Word in that way, to preach the cross of Christ for the life of the world. Luther was less concerned with parts of the Bible in which he saw nothing that pointed to Christ. He would have agreed with Francis' method of finding texts throughout the Bible which illuminated the passion of Christ.

Francis stands historically prior to our stereotypical distinction between Churches of the Word and Churches of the sacraments. It must be remembered that Francis was confronted by the Bible as it was read in the eucharistic assembly—at Mass. To the lectionary, the book of Sunday lessons, Francis listened for his life's direction. To the lectionary, Francis led Bernard. For Francis, the Bible was not a book which individuals own, read, and interpret, and by which they are consoled in the faith. After all, he lived in a time when Bibles were hand-copied and found only in great libraries. Most Christians heard the Word in the liturgy. They relied for their understanding of Scripture on hearing the lessons read in Latin and explained by the priest in the vernacular. For all his quoting of the Bible, Francis did not even own a Bible.

Although he was an itinerant preacher in the style of many contemporary Protestant evangelists, he should not be called a patron of individualistic biblical interpretation. Always it was the Gospels of the Church he recited; always on behalf of heightened reverence for the Eucharist he preached. In Francis, we see the stereotypes coming together: the preacher for the sake of the Church, the Eucharist for the sake of the Word.

It is not surprising that the Lutheran-Roman Catholic dialogues have occurred at a time of worship renewal and emerging liturgical consensus in both our traditions. In their rediscovery of the centrality of the Eucharist, Lutherans are preaching the Word in relation to the meal. In their renewal of preaching, Roman Catholics are giving more attention to the Word proclaimed in the liturgy.

A SIMPLE PROFUNDITY

A second matter requiring our attention is Francis' literal interpretation of the Scriptures. His method was not the usual one in the Middle Ages. It was more common to use allegorical interpretation to discern the meaning of the text. One relied on the wisdom of the Church Fathers in the difficult task of interpretation. To this day, we do not associate literal reading of the Bible with Roman Catholicism. Stereotypically, some of the Protestant Churches are described as encouraging literalism, the preacher opening the Bible and expounding literally upon the meaning of a verse selected at random. Francis was not interested in translating the meaning of a biblical text into a more palpable maxim for good living. The literal meaning of the open book was the meaning of the Bible for him.

Let us not suppose that Francis' literal hearing of the Word is the same thing as what we call modern fundamentalism. Francis was not concerned with some of our questions about meaning and historicity. Francis always asked whether the biblical text pointed to Christ crucified. The biblical passages which he prescribed for use at daily prayer relate the psalms to Christ in the same way as the responsories of the modern Roman breviary and the psalm prayers of the Lutheran Book of Worship. Francis' illustration of the manger as the eucharistic table sought to show, even at the crèche, Christ crucified. Similarly, Martin Luther's Christmas hymn "Vom Himmel Hoch" (From Heaven Above) has to do more with our change of life than with the cuteness of the Divine Infant. How different these examples are from some contemporary Christmas cards, pageants, and decorations which place the manger comfortably away from the cross.

RADICAL OBEDIENCE TO CHRIST

The matter of literal interpretation raises a third question: obedience to the commands of Christ. Mainline Christianity has frequently shied away from the conviction that a radically new lifestyle is incumbent upon the baptized Christian. In the ancient Church, before Christianity was first legal and then fashionable, the adult catechumenate, at least in some localities, seems to have taken quite seriously the radical reform of life as a prerequisite to baptism. Indeed, in the primitive Church there was even controversy about whether a baptized Christian could ever sin again. Early documents indicate the severe penances required should a Christian have committed a grave sin. When the Church became identified with the culture, such radicality was no longer expected—or even preached. Those who wished radical reform of life could enter the vowed religious life. Saints were, after all, saints, above and apart from the rest.

In some Reformation Churches, committed groups attempted radical lifestyles. Protestant utopian communities were modeled on descriptions of the Church in the Book of Acts. Geneva was John Calvin's attempt to create a city of God on earth. Lutheranism took a different approach. It respected the "orders of creation" as the established form of life on earth, and sought for renewal of heart within the context of structures already given. In Luther's distinction between Law and Gospel, the Gospel is the good news of God's grace that frees the faithful. Lutherans have tended to think of the radical demands of the New Testament as part of the law, the command of God which humans cannot possibly obey and from which the Gospel frees us. Thus they have avoided serious consideration of the radical commands which shaped Francis' discipleship.

Francis heard the Gospel mandates as directed to his person and obeyed them literally. Some Christians emulate him; others cannot; still others find such emulation inappropriate. We must recall some things about Francis before we make our own judgment. His literal hearing of the Word did not encourage him to live a solitary Christian life. He held no idiosyncratic theology or private views. Instead, his few extant letters are filled with pleas for his followers to be devoutly faithful to the Church, to give reverence to the clergy, and to obey the bishop. He took literally the command of Christ and left all to preach the Gospel, then did not rest until he received papal approval. His companions did not form a utopian community set off from the Church as somehow holier. Rather they were a community within the Church, called to preach penance to the wider community. For Francis remained overwhelmed by God's grace. Like the ancient Hebrews, Francis saw the call to obedience not as the antithesis of grace, but as a component of grace.

Contemporary Lutherans and Roman Catholics may find themselves closer to one another than to Francis on this matter. In general, we are not known either for our literal belief in the commands of Christ or for our evangelistic fervor. We are trying to survive in a "post-Christian" world. Perhaps this is why we temper radical obedience with exemptions that our reason finds suitable. Our missionary efforts are altered by sophisticated understanding of psychological states and knowledge of world religions. It would be good for Roman Catholics and Lutherans alike to share honestly their response to Francis' obedience to the Word and to question that response.

Not only did Francis believe the Word literally; he preached it simply. The influence of the "higher biblical criticism" during the last two hundred years and the role of theologians have made the spiritual life of both laity and clergy quite different from what it was in Francis' day. If being devout in the thirteenth century meant praying unceasingly or selling one's goods, today devout parishioners have the option of studying biblical commentaries and reading serious theological works. In Francis' spirit, however, there have always been groups in both our traditions who have sought the open book without scholarly assistance. Prayer gatherings, charismatic movements, service organizations, and Bible-study groups seek to confront God in the Word unmediated by sophisticated training in Scripture. Francis inspires us to find ways by which such movements can remain within the Church, not in its vestibule or away from it altogether. In a world in which biblical knowledge is diminishing, it is good merely to know the Bible more thoroughly and to revere its Word as a gift from God.

SHARING BIBLICAL RENEWAL

Together we join Francis in the task of preaching the open book. Visiting in one another's churches may help us to examine and evaluate our own proclamation. How is the Word read and preached? Could it be done more effectively? Has a neighboring parish a better way from which we can learn? Are the lessons read and expounded so that Christ is truly proclaimed? Do the lessons point to the Eucharist? We are endeavoring together to renew our proclamation, making it engaging, centering it on Christ, pointing it to eucharistic participation. We need one another's wisdom on what works and what does not.

One instance of our mutual renewal of biblical proclamation can be found in the new three-year lectionary. While not every lesson is the same, while the chronology is not always identical, and while some traditional celebrations are unique to one group or the other, we Lutherans and Roman Catholics have essentially the same Sunday readings, shared with Episcopalians, Presbyterians, and Methodists. Increasingly other Protestants are adopting the format. The amount of ecumenical sharing in this continuing process toward a single lectionary is astounding. Joint ecumenical committees of biblical scholars, liturgists, homilists, and theologians ask one another essential questions: What is the Gospel? What shall be read in the assembly? These are central questions for the Church, because the biblical passages read in the lectionary are for the most part the Bible that is known by the faithful. The day is not far off when we will meet, each in our own churches, to hear exactly the same biblical lessons read.

Finally, we should not omit a final question—or is it the first? Does the proclamation of Christ effect repentance and renewal? Does it produce repentance and renewal in me? Francis was no sectarian who preached sacrifice while driving a Mercedes. He continually upbraided himself for not completely heeding the Word of God. On occasion he went into the town square and confessed his sins aloud to anyone who would hear. He not only preached the open Bible unto conversion. He himself was converted and continued to seek conversion. In his very person he became a proclamation of the Word, a showing forth of Christ.

We pray the "psalm" from Francis' Fifth Office for the Christmas season:[14]

> Sing joyfully to God our strength; cry jubilee to the Lord, the true and living God, with a voice of exultation.
>
> For the Lord, the Most High, the awesome, is the great King over all the earth.
>
> Our most holy Father of heaven, our King, before time was, sent his beloved Son from on high and he was born of the blessed and holy Virgin Mary.
>
> He shall say of me, "You are my father," and I will make him the first-born, highest of the kings of the earth.
>
> By day the Lord bestows his grace, and at night I have his song.
>
> This is the day the Lord has made; let us be glad and rejoice in it.
>
> To our race this most holy and well loved son is given; for our sakes a child is born on the wayside and laid in a manger because there was no room for him in the inn.
>
> Glory to God in the highest, and on earth peace among men of good will.
>
> Let the heavens be glad and the earth rejoice; let the sea and what fills it resound; let the plains be joyful and all that is in them.

Sing to the Lord a new song; sing to the Lord, all you
lands.

For great is the Lord and highly to be praised; awe-
some is he, beyond all gods.

Give to the Lord, you families of nations, give to the
Lord glory and praise; give to the Lord the glory
due his name!

Prepare your hearts and take up his cross; live by his
holy commandments to the last.

3
His Work

Changed now perfectly in heart and soon to be changed in body too, Francis was walking one day near the church of St. Damian, which had nearly fallen to ruin and was abandoned by everyone. Led by the Spirit, he went in and fell down before the crucifix in devout and humble supplication; and smitten by unusual visitations, he found himself other than he had been when he entered. While he was thus affected, something unheard of before happened to him: the painted image of Christ crucified moved its lips and spoke. Calling him by name it said: "Francis, go, repair my house, which, as you see, is falling completely to ruin." Trembling, Francis was not a little amazed and became almost deranged by these words. He prepared himself to obey and gave himself completely to the fulfillment of this command. But since he felt that the change he had undergone was beyond expression, it is becoming that we should be silent about what he could not express. From then on compassion for the crucified was rooted in his holy soul, and, as it can be piously supposed, the stigmata of the venerable passion were deeply imprinted in his heart, though not as yet upon his flesh. . . .

He never forgot to be concerned about that holy image, and he never passed over its command with negligence. Right away he gave a certain priest some money that he might buy a lamp and oil, lest the sacred image should be deprived of the due honor of a light even for a moment. Then he diligently *hastened to do the rest and devoted his untiring efforts toward repairing that church. For, though the divine command concerned itself with the church that Christ had purchased with his own blood, Francis would not suddenly become perfect, but he was to pass gradually from the flesh to the spirit.*

The Second Life
(Thomas of Celano, 1246)[15]

RENEWER OF THE CHURCH

Francis did not set out to renew the Church. He rather resolved to obey as literally as he could the Word he personally received from God. The story tells that when Christ spoke to him from the crucifix in the decrepit church of St. Damian, Francis responded typically, simply, literally. He obtained money—this time by selling fabric from his father's store—and began to repair the little ruined chapel in which he heard the command of Christ.

The same was true concerning his decision about dress. He did not set out to design a distinctive religious habit for the thousands upon thousands who were to adopt his dress as their own. Instead, he heard the Gospel which said that everyone should own only one tunic, not even shoes for the feet, and he made his clothing as simple as possible. Already he was wearing a poor man's tunic with a leather belt. He discarded the belt for a simple cord. That cord has become a symbol of Church reform and renewal.

Four years after Francis heard the command to repair the church, the year after he donned the cord, he already had twelve followers. They were not men he personally evangelized, surely not men he recruited, but men from various stations of society who were inspired by Francis' example to dedicate themselves to his vision of Christ. They joined him, donned his sackcloth and cord, embraced Lady Poverty, and preached penance. With these twelve, Francis went to Rome to seek the blessing of Pope Innocent III. Francis saw his preaching not as peripheral to the Church's mainstream, but as one with its life. To be able to preach freely and to beg without harrassment, the little band of companions desired sanction from the Church, a sign of approval that their contribution to its life was valid.

The story is told that the Pope ignored this gang of beggars. That night, however, the Pope had a dream, a vision of himself in the deserted basilica of St. John Lateran, when the entire superstructure began to collapse around him. Then one man shoulders the pillars, rights them and saves the church. The Atlas is the ragged, barefoot pilgrim Francis. So the Pope gave the Franciscan Order his blessing, saying finally to his assembled court: "This is certainly the man who, by his work and teaching, will uphold the Church of Christ."[16]

Francis went, preaching the Word and renewing the Church. More and more men followed him. What shall they be called? Brothers, yes, but not, Francis hopes, like the Benedictines, whose brotherhood became rich in property and whose leaders ruled as abbots above the others. Francis' brotherhood was at root a lay movement and was dedicated to the simple life. "Little Brothers" was their name. Not until a generation after Francis' death, with the influx of many theologically trained clerics, did the communities begin to be filled with fathers—priests—rather than brothers. Eleven years after the Pope's approval, the famous General Chapter called the Chapter of Mats was attended by an estimated five thousand Little Brothers—so powerful was the influence of the little poor man and so desperate was the culture for renewal.

In that same year, the first formal Rule was promulgated. In it, Francis' desire for Church renewal is evident. Chapter I states the objective: the friars are to live following the teaching and footsteps of the Lord Jesus Christ. They are to wear poor clothes, a tunic and a cord. They are to pray the office, fast, work in the service of others, beg alms, evangelize unbelievers, and preach penance. That is, they are to be a sign of renewal in the Church. Their obligation, "to repair the Church," lies in repairing and reconstructing their own lives. Innocent III's dream was prophetic, because the Church will be upheld by the faith of those who are renewed in their commitment to Jesus Christ.

SECOND AND THIRD ORDERS

On Palm Sunday, a year after the Pope's dream, the first woman took the cord. Clare, a young noblewoman of Assisi, left home to assume a life of poverty. She was actually forced to seek asylum in the sanctuary, so vehement was her family in demanding her return from the disreputable life of the homeless, beggared gang. Not much later, the original group of Poor Clares was given a ruined church of its own to repair. In thirty years there were fifty women in this second Franciscan Order, living a cloistered life of poverty and prayer. Clare remained a close friend of Francis, but in a kind of mystical union required by their strict interpretation of the celibate life. Francis called her Christiana and urged the brothers not to think of the women as sisters, because the women were, in the first place, sisters of Jesus Christ. The story is told that once Francis and Clare ate a meal together outside and that, as they spoke together about their life in God, a great glow of light shone from the hillside as if people were seeing the fire of their love and the radiance of their sanctity.

The life of the Poor Clares is a different gift to the Church than is the life of the Little Brothers. Women could not, in those days, be mendicants, traveling beggars, or preachers. They were, instead, cloistered contemplatives, whose life was dedicated to prayer. Since they could not, because of their life-style, encounter Christ directly in their neighbor, they devoted themselves to Christ in the Eucharist. Clare is often pictured holding the bread of the Eucharist in a golden monstrance, Christ protecting the women with the words: "I will always defend you." The Poor Clares relied either on charity or on goods they received in exchange for the fine vestments and paraments they sewed.

Once when preaching in a small town named Poggibonsi, Francis was confronted by whole families who wanted to follow Christ in this new way. Francis realized that the rigorous requirements of the Little Brothers would not allow those families to become Franciscans. So he began a Third Franciscan Order, a secular Order, an Order of penance, in which lay people could join in a life of reconciliation and dedication to Christ. The Third Order has included many famous people: Elizabeth of Hungary (November 17, Lutheran Book of Worship and Roman Catholic calendars); the artists Giotto and Michelangelo; the musician Palestrina; the poet Dante; the statesman Thomas More; the scientist Michael Faraday; and more recently, folk-singer Arlo Guthrie.

There is a famous story told of a juggler who had no gift to offer the Christ Child, and so, when no one was looking, he juggled before a statue of the Virgin and Child. It is not surprising that this tale was associated with the Third Franciscan Order. Once the juggler shared a meal with some Little Brothers, and they reminded him that work done well in joy is done to the glory of God. So, artists and politicians, a princess and a juggler adopted the cord and wore it at their burial.

FORGIVENESS AND EUCHARIST

Another incident from Francis' life connects his interest in rebuilding ruined churches and his desire to renew the

Church. Francis and his companions had rebuilt the church of St. Mary of Portiuncola, a small chapel in which Francis had experienced some of his original visions and which the Benedictines had given him for a home. Francis went to the Pope and asked whether the penitents who came to visit this rebuilt chapel could receive a plenary indulgence—that is, full remission of the temporal punishment due to sin—without having to make any offering or perform any penitential act. Francis had already rebuilt a church building, but he was more concerned with rebuilding penitents, their souls, their lives. The Pope asked how many years of indulgence Francis sought, and the little poor man replied that he sought for the faithful full and complete remission of sins both on earth and in heaven. The Pope, convinced that Francis' request was inspired by Christ, granted it.

The Portiuncola Pardon was an extraordinary exception to the medieval system of penance which sought to take seriously God's justice by requiring from the faithful some proof of amendment of life. Francis surely epitomized such amendment, and the cord he adopted has come to symbolize the preaching of grace and forgiveness to penitents. Francis was never in the business of judging others or of pointing out faults. He considered himself the lowest of sinners, the poorest example of faith. Thus he asked that forgiveness be given to all, without prejudice, who like him sought God's mercy.

Another example of Francis' dedication to Church renewal is his reverence for the Eucharist. During his life he remained devoutly receptive to the sacrament, and he urged the same reverence on his hearers. He sought to become a missionary to France in order to preach reverence for Christ in the eucharistic elements. His letters repeatedly show his concern that the brothers receive Communion regularly and that priests show the necessary regard for the sacrament—Christ among us. In his final testament, Francis wrote: "I cannot see the most high Son of God with my own eyes, except for his most holy Body and Blood. . . . Above everything else, I want this most holy Sacrament to be honored and venerated, and reserved in places which are richly ornamented. . . ."[17] In nearly every letter extant from Francis' pen, we read some request to receive the Holy Supper fervently, with "the greatest possible reverence and honor."[18] Francis' concern that the eucharistic vessels be as fine as possible demonstrates both his intention literally to improve the churches of Christ and his devotion to such commitment—his reverence for the Christ of the Church.

DIACONAL AND LAY MINISTRIES

Recently, Roman Catholics and Lutherans, in commemoration of the 450th anniversary of the Augsburg Confession, joined in a discussion which probed their agreements and disagreements on understanding the ordained ministry. Consideration of Francis suggests a discussion of the other ministries in the Church—the life of vowed religious men and women, and the life of the laity—and, perhaps most important, the interrelationship of the various ministries within the Church. We must remember that Francis was not an ordained priest. His vision of the movement he began was not clerical. He did not gather a fraternity of priests. Instead he envisioned several different kinds of lay orders, the diversity a symbol of the Holy Spirit's diverse gifts within the Church.

Francis was a deacon. We know none of the personal details about how he undertook this ministry. The story of the Christmas crèche makes it clear that he served as deacon at that liturgy. In those days, the diaconate was a step toward priesthood. One could stop without prejudice at any step along the way and live accordingly. The same is true in contemporary Roman Catholicism. Thus, Francis' life also encourages us to examine the diaconate and vowed religious life.

Lutherans and Roman Catholics share a confusion concerning the diaconate today. In Roman Catholicism there is a renewed interest in the permanent diaconate. Permanent deacons are found in many dioceses, but they function differently from place to place. However, the situation is not without problems. The relationship of the diaconate and presbyterate (priesthood) is hazy and depends much on the attitude of the priests involved. The difference between the deacon and the committed lay person is also not very clear. In some countries, a shortage of priests has left deacons to do much of the ongoing work of the Church. In other countries, deacons tend to be married subordinates to parish priests. Roman Catholics are involved in continuing study of the diaconate.

The diaconate in Lutheranism is no less confusing. In some Lutheran churches, there are orders of deaconesses, dedicated women who are consecrated to a life of service. Seldom have the deaconesses had much visibility in the North American churches. Until recently, they have not had the historic role of liturgical deacon. Some synods have begun deacon programs, offering several years of study in the Bible and practical skills, after which graduate deacons serve in a great variety of ways. But some Lutheran parishes use the term deacon quite differently, as a title for a church officer who helps direct the affairs of a local congregation. The Lutheran Book of Worship uses "assisting minister" instead of "deacon" for the secondary leader at liturgy. Furthermore, it is urged that such liturgical assistants be lay people, trained for the task, not clerics.

Lutheran deaconesses are traditionally more akin to medieval nuns than to modern deacons. In Lutheranism, vowed communities of deaconesses were first mostly communities of nurses or teachers and only more recently individual women linked by common commitment to the Church and employed in whatever way their life suggested. Both in North America and Europe a limited number of monastic orders have been re-established under Lutheran auspices in recent decades. But there is still a poor understanding of and considerable suspicion of the vowed religious life among many Lutherans.

As a result of the Second Vatican Council, religious communities in Roman Catholicism have shown increased commitment to renewal. They are examining the charisms of their founders and seeking to discover the meaning of the vowed life in the contemporary world.

DIVERSITY OF GIFTS

Thus we are led to many questions. What structures shall the Church recognize as most helpful for individual commitment and most beneficial for the whole Church? Should there be fewer or more designated ministries? What is the goal and effect of lay associations? Is Francis' Third Order of penance a model for the wider Church? How can the Church have various ministries without a hierarchy or rank? The Reformation criticized clerical domination and the privileges of monks, friars, and nuns. While eventually eliminating the vowed religious life, it held high the status of the ordained ministers. In some Lutheran traditions, one finds a subservience to the local pastor in a way that belies Reformation emphasis on lay vocation. Other Lutherans have put considerable emphasis on lay preaching as a supplement to clerical sermons.

Let us look at the interrelationship between the ministries which exist in the Church. Francis was always eager to receive ecclesiastical blessing on his activities. He sought the Pope's approval, he submitted his Rule for sanction, and he urged friars never to preach itinerantly without the bishop's approval. The various ministries were to function differently, diversely, but not in conflict with one another. What is the unique vocation of the ordained minister, the lay person, the deacon, the

deaconess, the monk, the friar, the nun? How do these ministries receive and bless one another? How can the ministries
best complement one another? Can responsibilities be varied
without privileges of rank intervening? The vigor of all our
ministries lies in faithfulness to a unique vision of service to the
Church.

A third matter to re-examine is lay vocation. We turn to
Francis' establishment of a secular order for inspiration. The
Third Franciscan Order provides a Church-wide network for a
wide diversity of lay people to make a commitment to Franciscan ideals. Francis had no idea that only ordained people could
serve God. In fact, when families enthusiastically volunteered
to join his movement, he restrained them. Very much like Luther, he urged people to remain as they were, praising God,
serving their neighbors, and showing mercy in their daily vo-
cations. The Third Franciscan Order assists lay people to be
what they are—Christians committed to their lay role. Laity
need to testify to one another and to the world that the lay vocation is a primary one, secondary to none in the Church. We
are all, as Vatican II said, the people of God. We all share, said
Luther, in the priesthood of believers. Yet we must find better
ways to strengthen lay people in their vocation as baptized
Christians, especially as the world grows increasingly pagan.
The recent establishment of the "Laos in Ministry" movement
among Lutherans is one such attempt to do this.

WAYS OF REBUILDING

"Go, repair my church," Francis heard Jesus say. A fourth
point raised by Francis is a literal repairing of our churches.
We must rebuild buildings which seat too many, are too expensive to heat, are inaccessible to wheelchairs, are wildly clut-
tered with inferior religious art, are not well arranged for our
liturgies. For all of Francis' scorn of money, he always seemed

to find the gold necessary to make eucharistic vessels. His embrace of sackcloth did not suggest to him that church buildings should be mean, cheap and plain. The contemporary Church is involved in just such questions. How much money should be spent on buildings when, perhaps across the street, people are hungry? How specialized should a church edifice be? Should it be a place for community events or be used for worship alone? Our different traditions have different emphases to bring to such considerations. Perhaps by cooperating more with one another we can share enough resources to keep gold in the churches *and* give it away to the poor.

It has been suggested that because there is one baptism, one washing in which we all share, each locality should have one baptismal font, *the* Christian font for that place. Is this a legitimate "repair" of Christ's Church? (In one midwestern university town, while the Lutherans were "repairing their church," they used the ten o'clock hour at the Roman Catholic church next door. The liturgies were so much alike that the confused college students ended up worshiping at the "wrong" service. Is this a legitimate "repair" of Christ's Church?)

A fifth discussion point lies in Francis' call for reverence for the sacrament. Here again, although our traditions have made our histories different, our perspectives on the question are complementary. Francis means reverence for the sacrament both in faithful reception of it and in devotion to it. The painful truth is that participation in the weekly Eucharist does not necessarily mean having a profound reverence for the sacrament. Of course neither does abstinence—such as those Lutheran pietists who communed four times a year (or even less often) "to keep it special." In our day a growing concern for the use of real bread and abundant wine is contrasted with an older piety in which the consecrated bread and wine were so revered that the bread was unrecognizably special and (in Roman Catholic practice) the wine withheld. How to revere the sacramental food, how to share devotedly in the meal, how to act out our common assertion that Christ is truly present— these are liturgical questions that contemporary Lutherans and Roman Catholics share. Our belief that Christ's body and blood are present in the sacrament is one of the doctrinal bonds holding us together; we stand with Francis in this matter. It was not some bizarre magic that held Francis to the sacrament; rather it was Christ. So too with us.

Another issue raised by Francis' adoption of the cord and his repair of the Church is the connection between these two acts. It was not, we said, that Francis decided to renew the life of the Church. He certainly did not imagine himself as some heroic saint or mythological Atlas, supporting the Church of God. Rather he amended his life. He donned the sackcloth and wore the cord. He repaired one ruined church, and then another. From the cord, from the repairs, we see a vast harvest: ministries born, entire orders formed, major spiritual emphases embodied, even our current dialogue, planted by the cord of Francis. This is not to suggest that we do not need great plans and overarching schemes, huge fund drives for the strengthening of the foundations, long-range projects toward renewal and reconciliation. Rather it is to say that when a believer hears the call, the individual should obey it. In Francis we have an astounding model of one who by individual obedience inaugurated widespread renewal of the universal Church.

Finally, we must ask whether, or how much, the present repair of the Church means to reconciliation of denominations. Because most of the brokenness of the Church lies in its fragmentation into exclusive denominations, Francis urges us: Pick up some stones! Mix the mortar! Rebuild! We might think in this way of every Lutheran/Roman Catholic dialogue: we are two bricks which need to be more carefully cemented together in the continuous task of repairing Christ's Church. We are rebuilding ourselves, we, the walls of Jerusalem. Perhaps Francis' cord can tie us together in renewal of the Church.

We pray one of Francis' prayers:[19]

> Almighty, eternal, just and merciful God, grant us in our misery that we may do for your sake alone what we know you want us to do, and always want what pleases you, so that, cleansed and enlightened interiorly and fired with the ardor of the Holy Spirit, we may be able to follow in the footsteps of your Son, our Lord Jesus Christ, and so make our way to you, Most High, by your grace alone, you who live and reign in perfect Trinity and simple Unity, and are glorified, God all-powerful, for ever and ever. Amen.

4
His Friends

At a time when St. Francis was staying in the town of Gubbio, something wonderful and worthy of lasting fame happened.

For there appeared in the territory of that city a fearfully large and fierce wolf which was so rabid with hunger that it devoured not only animals but even human beings. All the people in the town considered it such a great scourge and terror—because it often came near the town—that they took weapons with them when they went into the country, as if they were going to war. But even with their weapons they were not able to escape the sharp teeth and raging hunger of the wolf when they were so unfortunate as to meet it. Consequently everyone in the town was so terrified that hardly anyone dared go outside the city gate.

But God wished to bring the holiness of St. Francis to the attention of those people.

For while the Saint was there at that time, he had pity on the people and decided to go out and meet the wolf. But on hearing this the citizens said to him: "Look out, Brother Francis. Don't go outside the gate, because the wolf which has already devoured many people will certainly attack you and kill you!"

But St. Francis placed his hope in the Lord Jesus Christ who is master of all creatures. Protected not by a shield or a helmet, but arming himself with the Sign of the Cross, he *bravely went out of the town with his companion, putting all his faith in the Lord who makes those who believe in Him walk without any injury on an asp and a basilisk and trample not merely on a wolf but even on a lion and a dragon. So with his very great faith St. Francis bravely went out to meet the wolf.*

Some peasants accompanied him a little way, but soon they said to him: "We don't want to go any farther because that wolf is very fierce and we might get hurt."

When he heard them say this, St. Francis answered: "Just stay here. But I am going on to where the wolf lives."

Then, in the sight of many people who had come out and climbed onto places to see this wonderful event, the fierce wolf came running with its mouth open toward St. Francis and his companion.

The Saint made the Sign of the Cross toward it. And the power of God, proceeding as much from himself as from his companion, checked the wolf and made it slow down and close its cruel mouth.

Then calling to it, St. Francis said: "Come to me, Brother Wolf. In the name of Christ, I order you not to hurt me or anyone."

It is marvelous to relate that as soon as he had made the Sign of the Cross, the wolf closed its terrible jaws and stopped running, and as soon as he gave it that order, it lowered its head and lay down at the Saint's feet, as though it had become a lamb.

And St. Francis said to it as it lay in front of him: "Brother Wolf, you have done great harm in this region, and you have committed horrible crimes by destroying God's creatures without any mercy. You not only have been destroying irrational animals, but you even have had the more detestable brazenness to kill and devour human beings made in the image of God. You therefore deserve to be put to death just like the worst robber and murderer. Consequently everyone is right in crying out against you and complaining, and this whole town is your enemy. But, Brother Wolf, I want to make peace between you and them, so that they will not be harmed by you any more, and after they have forgiven you all your past crimes, neither men nor dogs will pursue you any more."

The wolf showed by moving its body and tail and ears and by nodding its head that it willingly accepted what the Saint had said and would observe it.

So St. Francis spoke again: "Brother Wolf, since you are willing to make and keep this peace pact, I promise you that I will have the people of this town give you food every day as long as you live, so that you will never again suffer from hunger, for I know that whatever evil you have been doing was done because of the urge of hunger. But, my Brother Wolf, since I am obtaining such a favor for you, I want you to promise me that you will never hurt any animal or man. Will you promise me that?"

The wolf gave a clear sign, by nodding its head, that it promised to do what the Saint asked.

And St. Francis said: "Brother Wolf, I want you to give me a pledge so that I can confidently believe what you promise."

And as St. Francis held out his hand to receive the pledge, the wolf also raised its front paw and meekly and gently put it in St. Francis' hand as a sign that it was giving its pledge.

Then St. Francis said: "Brother Wolf, I order you, in the name of the Lord Jesus Christ, to come with me now, without fear, into the town to make this peace pact in the name of the Lord."

And the wolf immediately began to walk along beside St. Francis, just like a very gentle lamb. When the people saw this, they were greatly amazed, and the news spread quickly throughout the whole town, so that all of them, men as well as women, great and small, assembled in the market place, because St. Francis was there with the wolf.

So when a very large crowd had gathered, St. Francis gave them a wonderful sermon.... And then he added, "Listen, dear people. Brother Wolf, who is standing here before you, has promised me and has given me a pledge that he will make peace with you and will never hurt you if you promise also to feed him every day. And I pledge myself as bondsman for Brother Wolf that he will faithfully keep this peace pact."

Then all the people who were assembled there promised in a loud voice to feed the wolf regularly....

And St. Francis said: "Brother Wolf, just as you gave me a pledge of this when we were outside the city gate, I want you to give me a pledge here before all these people that you will keep the pact and will never betray me for having pledged myself as your bondsman."

Then in the presence of all the people the wolf raised its right paw and put it in St. Francis' hand as a pledge....

From that day, the wolf and the people kept the pact which St. Francis made. The wolf lived two years more, and it went from door to door for food. It hurt no one, and no one hurt it. The people fed it courteously. And it is a striking fact that not a single dog ever barked at it.

Then the wolf grew old and died. And the people were sorry, because whenever it went through the town, its peaceful kindness and patience reminded them of the virtues and the holiness of St. Francis.

Little Flowers of St. Francis
(ca. 1375)[20]

BROTHER OF NATURE

Chances are that if you have a depiction of Francis in your home, he is surrounded by woodland creatures, and that the last time you saw a statue of Francis, it was near a birdbath.

However, as one might guess, the stories of Francis and the animals have a depth which goes beyond mere cheap plaster casts.

The story is told that once when Francis was outdoors preaching to the townspeople, a flock of swallows were making such a racket that his words could not be heard. So he called to them that they had done enough talking for a while and that it was his turn to talk and their turn to listen to God's Word. Immediately they stopped their singing and settled down to listen to the preacher.

Francis called the creatures, the whole creation in fact, his brothers and sisters. Sister swallows quieted down when the saint preached the Gospel; he said that their song also praised God, just as do the loving actions of the faithful. Francis, that fine troubadour, once had a song contest with a nightingale, an antiphonal praise shared by man and bird; he judged in the end that the nightingale won. Francis had a pet crow, the story goes, who woke him in time for Matins; after his death, the crow guarded his tomb and died there of lonely grief. Even a cricket became a personal friend to Francis who said its clacking voice also praised God. The story says that Francis gathered around him wild creatures who were suddenly tamed by his presence; he preached to them, as to human beings, that they must praise God for the continuous gift of life and sustenance.

Francis had a special affection for lambs, because the Scriptures use the gentleness and meekness of the lamb as a type of Christ. Once he bought two lambs from a man who was delivering them to market for slaughter; he was filled with compassion for these weak creatures who were to suffer through no fault of their own. Another time he came upon a lamb being butted about in a herd of goats; he rescued it and delivered it to a convent so that it might live in security.

Lest we think that Francis cared only for cute animals, the

stories remind us that when he saw worms on the path, he would gently place them back in the grass so travelers would not inadvertently crush them. And it was not only animals, cute or not-so-cute, with whom Francis experienced a remarkable affinity. He urged his companions, in collecting firewood, never to cut down an entire tree, because the tree must be able to continue living and growing. The stories tell that in coming upon a field of flowers, he preached to them, reminding them that their beauty is a gift from God, their bloom a praise to the divine name. The sun and the moon, the stars and the clouds, are brothers and sisters as well.

The tale is told that when doctors concurred that Francis should have the veins on the side of his face, near his increasingly painful eye, cauterized, Francis spoke to the fire. His agonized eyes looked at the red-hot branding iron, and he said, "My brother fire, that surpasses all other things in beauty, the Most High created you strong, beautiful, and useful. Be kind to me in this hour, be courteous. For I have loved you in the past in the Lord. I beseech the great Lord who made you that he temper your heat now so that I may bear it when you burn me gently."[21] Indeed, when the cauterizing was over, the Saint claimed to have felt no pain. One stanza of the famous Canticle to Brother Sun recalls that fire; another speaks gentle words even to Sister Death, also a servant of God working for the purpose of salvation.

Finally there came the October night when Francis died. Thomas of Celano writes of that evening:

> The larks are birds that love the noonday light and shun the darkness of twilight. But on the night that St. Francis went to Christ, they came to the roof of the house, though already the twilight of the night to follow had fallen, and they flew about the house for a

long time amid a great clamor, whether to show their joy or their sadness in their own way by their singing, we do not know. Tearful rejoicing and joyful sorrow made up their song, either to bemoan the fact that they were orphaned children, or to announce that their father was going to his eternal glory. The city watchmen who guarded the place with great care were filled with astonishment and called the others to witness the wonder.[22]

BOUND BY COMPASSION

Let us try to understand what unique emphasis can be found in Francis' love of creation. It is not merely that he cared for cute animals, a kind of precursor to Walt Disney, or that he was concerned about endangered species. Nor was he scientifically interested in ecological balance, thus encouraging wildlife preservation and unpolluted air. Perhaps all that would be enough; with Francis there is more.

Bonaventure writes that it was Francis' great compassion which bound him to the creatures of nature. "It was loving compassion . . . which led him to devote himself humbly to his neighbor and enabled him to return to the state of primeval innocence by restoring man's harmony with the whole of creation."[23] The word that Bonaventure uses for compassion includes love, devotion, reverence, and kindness. Francis' humility before God kept him from any sense of superiority over the bird or the worm. His love for all creatures caused him to save the lamb from death. He stood humbly before the whole creation as before the realm of God.

One of Francis' emphases was that all of nature was, like him, created by God. He reminded the animals that God had given them life, invented their song, designed their loveliness. God had created the fire to be terrifyingly beautiful. Even death serves a purpose of God. Along with our Jewish fellow-believers, the Church has always taught that God created the world. The controversy over teaching creationism in public schools can be instructive. Of course, scientific theories of the origins of the universe, even while postulating complicated patterns of development, usually have a blank at the very beginning. Whence came the original cell, the original matter, the original force? It is not the purpose of Genesis to give a scientific answer to that question. Genesis lets God be God, the Creator, and calls for the human responses—praise. After all, the Bible includes several different stories of the formation of the universe. There is one version in Genesis 1, another in Genesis 2, and poetic versions in Psalm 74 and Job 26. Each biblical version agrees with Francis by offering a religious response—praise—to our search for origins.

For Francis, the belief that God created the universe implied that all creation is endowed with the gift of God's life. Francis did not expound on the unique qualities of the human being, on our vast distance from the rest of creation. Rather, God's creativeness provided the link which bound Francis as like with like to the good earth. The life of the lamb was valuable, the life of the worm was valuable, as was Francis' own, because they were gifts from God.

Another issue suggests itself, asked perenially by children: Will my pet cat get to heaven? What do we tell our children at the death of a pet? Do we actually believe what we tell them? What do we mean by the assertion that God is saving the whole created order? What do we mean by the word "soul"? In a recent best seller, *The White Hotel* by D. M. Thomas, there is a cat in paradise, and although spayed, she gives birth to a litter of healthy kittens! What do we think?

UNIVERSAL PRAISE

A second major emphasis of Francis was that all creation at its best is praising God. Not only is the human being called to offer praise. The birds' songs, the sun's light, the colors of the flowers, the work of the bees—all are responses to the Creator's love. As a child draws a self-portrait for her mother, so the universe offers itself in praise. The sermons in which we overhear Francis preaching to the animals say that the animals praise God by being their best living selves.

Joyful response to the creation in praise of the Creator has been a strong emphasis in Roman Catholicism. The Scholastic theology which we associate with Thomas Aquinas and Bonaventure taught the goodness of God in creation. Grace cooperates with nature—that is, the goodness that we know of God in Christ is a logical extension of the goodness of God we see in the created order. God's salvation is not something different from God's creation. In all God's actions, we experience divine grace.

Because nature has been imbued with goodness by God, one can talk about the creation's response to God. The sun's rays, the flower's color, the bird's song are not only natural phenomena, but also praises to God. Most significantly, there is a way to speak about the effective response of the graced human being. People graced by God can serve faithfully. There is a life of growth in grace. It is not surprising that one of the differences between Roman Catholic and Lutheran eucharistic piety lies in the meaning of the preparation of the gifts, which used to be called the offertory of the Mass. There is no question in the Roman Catholic tradition that the faithful have much to offer, themselves along with the eucharistic gifts of bread and wine.

The Lutheran emphasis has frequently been different. The Reformation was intent on maintaining that the unique and only necessary gift of God is Christ. Since Luther sought to stress that salvation is *pro me*, for me, he did not talk so much about God's goodness in creation. Besides, since Bonaventure, the Western Church had lived through the black plague and the Avignon papacy; it was not so evident any longer that the creation was good and that the Church was an offering. Lutheranism focused on God's gift of Christ for the human being; thus some Lutherans talk less of the goodness of nature. While one cannot point to classic arguments concerning creation between Roman Catholics and Lutherans, one does find a difference in emphasis. While Lutherans affirm the goodness of creation, they quickly remind themselves that the good of salvation is in Christ alone.

Understandably, then, Lutherans have not talked easily about offering, because the things of nature, including human beings, are not seen as having much to offer God. In the beloved hymn "Beautiful Savior," nature is seen as less exalted than Jesus. It is interesting that in one Lutheran hymnal there are two versions of a hymn entitled "Oh That I Had a Thousand Voices." In one version, the grasses, trees and animals join to praise God; this hymn is in the "Praise" section of the book. The other, located in the "Trinity" section, recounts the saving work of God in Christ for us. Originally, these were not two ideologically separated hymns; rather, all the stanzas were part of one even longer German chorale. But it is not surprising that much Lutheran piety found it more authentic to sing of Christ "for me" than to sing praise with the grass and clouds.

More significant are the ramifications of the Lutheran discomfort with the idea of offering. The Reformation theme that Holy Communion is the gift of God has made the contemporary emphasis on Eucharist as thanksgiving and on the prayer of thanksgiving as an offering of praise seem strange to many Lutherans. Surely much more sharing between our two traditions on this point is necessary. The Church needs to remember both that only through Christ's gift are we saved, and that God has brought forth a good creation which can offer its praise.

INCARNATIONAL PEOPLE

Lest these differences make us feel quite distant from one another, a third point must be stressed. Both Roman Catholicism and Lutheranism are incarnational at heart. In many religions—and in some Christian pieties—the things of God are so holy, so far beyond created things, that there is a great gulf fixed between the sacred and secular. Religion thus means the painful effort in which the secular scales the sacred ladder, or jumps the gulf, or mystically merges with what is distinctly other. Neither Lutheranism nor Roman Catholicism has encouraged such a theology or piety. We are incarnational people—that is, we believe that God became incarnate, took human flesh, in the person of Jesus. By the merging of the divine and the human all the created order is viewed differently. Because the gulf has been bridged, we are also sacramental people. Just as God entered humanity in Jesus Christ, so God enters the created order. God is in the water of baptism; God is in the elements of Communion; God is in the sound waves of preaching. While our traditions may deal in different ways with God's presence in the natural order, together we affirm that God's world is good, that God saved the world by joining it in Christ, and that God enters the created order to save the world sacramentally.

Because of incarnation, we value nature. Because God created the world, because the whole world is being redeemed, because all creation can offer praise to God, we are concerned about the environment. It is common to quote Genesis 1 when we speak of the relationship between human beings and the created order: "Fill the earth and subdue it." Under a divine mandate Christians, like many other people, have cut down forests to build more homes. The time is here when few forests remain, so we listen to Genesis 2, which tells how God placed Adam in a garden and created all the animals in an attempt to find a suitable companion for man. In local communities, an ecological project suggests itself as a vehicle for joint Lutheran/Roman Catholic efforts, in compassion for creation and in remembrance of Francis.

The best known writing of Francis is his Canticle of Brother Sun. A contemporary translation is offered here for our joint prayer. But first a word about Francis' Umbrian dialect. In many stanzas Francis used ambiguous prepositions, such as *cum* and *per:* "Laudato si, misignore, *cum* . . ." and "Laudato si, misignore, *per* . . ." These prepositions can mean different things. We could translate: "All praise be yours for all your creation." That is, we are grateful that God has created such a diverse, productive world. Or "per" could mean "through": "All praise be yours, my Lord, through moon and wind and fire"— that is, the world unconsciously, perhaps, gives praise as it lives out its intended usefulness. A popular versified translation (*Lutheran Book of Worship,* 527; *Worship* II, 8) translates these troublesome prepositions as "by": God is praised *by* the creation. Thus the direction of the hymn is reversed; it addresses, not God, but the creatures themselves, asking them to praise God. Francis' anniversary is a good time to popularize this hymn, "All Creatures of Our God and King." Unfortunately, this is not the most accurate translation. Francis is not talking to the birds. Other translations use the preposition "in," as if God is in everything and we praise God in the wind. This is an unacceptable pantheism, a heresy for Christians.

In the translation used here, Francis' aim is clear. The recurring "All praise be yours" demonstrates repeatedly that the canticle is in praise of God. Indeed, not only does humankind praise the Creator, but all creation as well, even death itself.

The final lines repeat one of Francis' constant themes: Why
this affinity with nature? Because we "serve him with great
humility." It is important, finally, to note that Francis did not
write his canticle while romping through the fields in midsum-
mer. He wrote it a year before his death, in midwinter, while
in great pain. He was nearly blind, undergoing excruciating
head pains, and suffering from several debilitating intestinal
disorders. His praise came from his total submission to God—
all was praise of God—not from some romantic notion of how
lovely birds looked.

We pray the Canticle of Brother Sun:[24]

> Most high, all-powerful, all good, Lord!
>> All praise is yours, all glory, all honor
>> And all blessing.
> To you, alone, Most High, do they belong.
>> No mortal lips are worthy
>> To pronounce your name.
> All praise be yours, my Lord, through all that you have
>> made,
>> And first my lord Brother Sun,
>> Who brings the day; and light you give to us
>>> through him.
> How beautiful is he, how radiant in all his splendor!
>> Of you, Most High, he bears the likeness.
> All praise be yours, my Lord, through Sister Moon and
>> Stars;
>> In the heavens you have made them, bright
>> And precious and fair.
> All praise be yours, my Lord, through Brothers Wind
>> and Air,
>> And fair and stormy, all the weather's moods,
>> By which you cherish all that you have made.

All praise be yours, my Lord, through Sister Water,
>   So useful, lowly, precious and pure.
All praise be yours, my Lord, through Brother Fire,
>   Through whom you brighten up the night.
>   How beautiful is he, how gay! Full of power and
>   strength.
All praise be yours, my Lord, through Sister Earth, our
    mother,
>   Who feeds us in her sovereignty and produces
>   Various fruits with colored flowers and herbs.
All praise be yours, my Lord, through those who grant
    pardon
>   For love of you; through those who endure
>   Sickness and trial.
Happy those who endure in peace;
>   By you, Most High, they will be crowned.
All praise be yours, my Lord, through Sister Death,
>   From whose embrace no mortal can escape.
Woe to those who die in mortal sin!
>   Happy those she finds doing your will!
>   The second death can do no harm to them.
Praise and bless my Lord, and give him thanks,
>   And serve him with great humility.

5
His Befriending

At the time when Francis was very sick—the "Praises of the Lord" had already been composed—the bishop of Assisi excommunicated the podesta. In return, the podesta had it announced to the sound of the trumpet in the streets of the city that every citizen was forbidden to buy from or sell anything whatsoever to the bishop or to transact any business with him. There was a savage hatred between them. Blessed Francis, who was very sick at that time, pitied them. It pained him to see that no one, religious or lay, intervened to re-establish peace and concord between them. So he said to his companions: "It is a great shame for us, the servants of God, that at a time when the podesta and the bishop so hate each other no one can be found to re-establish peace and concord between them!" On this occasion he added the following strophe to his canticle:

> All praise be yours, my Lord,
> Through those who grant pardon for love of you;
> Through those who endure sickness and trial.
> Happy those who endure in peace;
> By you, Most High, they will be crowned.

He then called one of his companions and said to him: "Go and find the podesta and tell him for me that he should go to the bishop's palace with the notables of the commune and with

61

all those he can assemble." When the brother had left, he said to the others: "Go, and in the presence of the bishop, of the podesta, and of the entire gathering, sing the Canticle of Brother Sun. I have confidence that the Lord will put humility and peace in their hearts and that they will return to their former friendship and affection."

When everyone had gathered at the place of the cloister of the bishop's palace, the two brothers stood up, and one of them was the spokesman. He said: "Despite his sufferings, blessed Francis has composed the 'Praises of the Lord' for all his creatures, to the praise of God and for the edification of his neighbor; he asks you to listen with great devotion."

With that, they began to sing. The podesta stood up and joined his hands as for the Gospel of the Lord, and he listened with great recollection and attention; soon tears flowed from his eyes, for he had a great deal of confidence in blessed Francis and devotion for him. At the end of the canticle, the podesta cried out before the entire gathering: "In truth I say to you, not only do I forgive the lord bishop whom I ought to recognize as my master, but I would even pardon my brother's and my own son's murderer!" He then threw himself at the feet of the lord bishop and said to him: "For the love of our Lord Jesus Christ and of blessed Francis, his servant, I am ready to make any atonement you wish." The bishop stood up and said to him: "My office demands humility of me, but by nature I am quick to anger; you must forgive me!" With much tenderness and affection, both locked arms and embraced each other.

The brothers were in admiration to see that the sanctity of blessed Francis had fulfilled to the letter what he had said of the peace and concord to be restored between these two men. All who witnessed the scene ascribed the grace so promptly given to the two adversaries to a miracle due to the merits of the saint. These two men, forgetting all past offensive words *and after a very great scandal, returned to a very great concord.*

Legend of Perugia
(Brother Leo, ca. 1270)[25]

PEACEMAKER FOR GOD

The story of the reconciliation of the bishop and the mayor of Assisi illustrates one of Francis' extraordinary gifts: peacemaking. It is useful here to recall what Francis' world was like. He grew up in a town embroiled in civil war. All the classes and estates were violently seeking to become ascendant in the emerging European economy. When Assisi stopped fighting internally, it began fighting its neighbors. Physical brutality was commonplace—noses cut off defeated soldiers, women raped. Torture and revenge were part of the war games between quarreling cities. Blatant person-to-person atrocities are difficult for us to understand, so far we think we have come from such a conduct of war.

Not only was Francis surrounded by battles, but until his mid-twenties he accepted warfare as his life. He fought in Assisi's army against Perugia. He was a prisoner-of-war for a year. He headed off to the courts of Count Gautier to serve in his ranks of knights. Then he first heard Christ tell him to return home for a different life. In viewing this bellicose background, it is not surprising that his early biographers emphasize Francis' mission of peace. Thomas of Celano writes, "In all his preaching, before he proposed the Word of God to those gathered about, he first prayed for peace for them, saying, 'The Lord give you peace.' He always most devoutly announced peace to men and women, to all he met and overtook. For this reason, many who had hated peace and had hated also salvation embraced peace, through the cooperation of the Lord, with all their heart and were made children of peace and seekers after eternal salvation."[26] *"Pax et bonum"* was the greeting Francis taught his companions. They became heralds of the king of peace, and the world listened. Stories abound that when the simple sackclothed men stood in village squares, and preached peace, soldiers left the ranks, quarrels were forgotten, and war was abandoned.

There was something personally transformative about Francis. Once when he was absent from Italy, his order began quarreling over rights, powers and interpretations. Francis returned home quickly to make peace among his companions. His taming the wolf of Gubbio suggests that his powers of reconciliation were effective even with wild animals. In his person as well as in his preaching, he was able to relate for people the reconciliation we find in Christ and the reconciliation we grant our neighbor.

Perhaps the most famous tale of Francis in this regard is his visit to the sultan. This was no pleasure jaunt. The Crusades were raging. Europe's devout Christians were intent on regaining the Holy Land. The inhumanity of the battles is difficult for contemporary minds to fathom. Francis was distraught by the overwhelming cruelty which Christians and Muslims were inflicting on one another. A decisive event had just occurred—the city of Damietta had been taken by Christians, and a pitiful victory it was. When finally stormed, the walled fortress was a city of corpses, the soldiers dead, the population starved. It took the Christians only a short time to recover from the tragedy of that battle, because looting quickly began. In the Holy Land it was a fight to the death. No Christian was safe in the presence of a Muslim; no Muslim was safe in the presence of a Christian.

In this situation, Francis decided to preach to the Muslim sultan. Some people suggest that since it was so likely that these evangelizing Franciscans would be killed, the venture must have been an attempt to seek martyrdom. There is no doubt that Francis was taken with the glorious possibilities of dying for the faith. His conduct before the sultan hardly suggests someone who is choosing death, however. In fact, he proposed a duel in which he would gladly enter flames to prove the lordship of Christ. Would one of the sultan's servants do the same for his God? It is unlikely that Francis would have suggested such a contest as a vindication of his God had he not been convinced of God's protection.

The story says that the sultan was intrigued by this ragged barefoot preacher, fascinated by his naiveté, and amazed by his religious courage. The sultan entertained Francis and his companion for several weeks. Eventually he gave Francis safe conduct back to the weary Christian army with an escort of Saracen knights fit for an emperor.

The story of Francis' preaching to the sultan illustrates Francis' commitment to proclamation of the Word. Perhaps more than that, it stands as a witness to his powers of reconciliation. It is hardly surprising that his preaching did not convert the sultan. It is, however, astonishing that Francis lived through the adventure and returned safely home. In the midst of some of the most vindictive, brutal warfare that Western history has known, these two leaders had some days of conversation, a space for reconciliation in the center of the fray. Tradition tells that the ivory horn which lies among the relics of Francis in the basilica at Assisi was a gift to Francis from the sultan who had used it to call his troops into battle. Francis used it to call his companions to prayer. The trumpet of battle given in friendship became an Angelus bell.

THE WEAPONS OF PEACE

Francis thus became a symbol of reconciliation. The peacemaker who stood untouched by warfare around him is still invoked as one who shows the way of peace. The popular prayer "Lord, make me an instrument of your peace, that where there is hatred, let me show love . . ." was not actually composed by Francis. It is logical, though, that a poetic prayer for peace would be associated with this humble man riding headlong into a Muslim camp intent on preaching to the sultan, this dying friar who sent his companions to sing a song to a bishop and mayor embroiled in bitter controversy.

It is interesting to speculate how Francis was able to effect peace wherever he went. It is easiest to see ways he did not. He did not attempt to compromise. He knew exactly what he believed. While he was humble and gentle in bearing, he did not hesitate to speak his convictions. The first gift he gave for repair of a ruined church was obtained by selling goods from his father's store. The resulting quarrel led to his father's suing him before the bishop's court and to Francis' rejection of his father. There is no evidence that this fight was ever happily resolved. For Francis, making peace did not imply companionship born of lack of individual conviction.

Francis could be a harbinger of peace even though he knew he was right. He is no model of interfaith dialogue. He was not in the least interested in hearing and understanding the sultan's religious views. He was not a waffler who became a friend because he condoned every opinion. He was no twentieth-century relativist. Yet, although he unremittingly tried to convert the sultan, he was able to be a person of peace.

Francis did not effect peace in an ordinary—though paradoxical—way by showing force. A popular contemporary assumption about how the world powers should make peace holds that they must boldly demonstrate their fighting capabilities. The proudest cock of the walk is not attacked. Surely it was not by any power of his learning or his bearing or his position or his possessions that Francis became a sign of peace, because of these he had none.

We are left with the old biographies which without complicated psychological and social analyses merely tell us that Francis achieved reconciliation wherever he went. His humility confronted the pride which quarreling requires. His genuineness made people realize their own bravado. His naiveté opened up their complicated facades. His absolute poverty was an indictment of the worlds over which battles were fought. As Francis said to the Pope in explaining his vision for the Franciscan Order, those who own nothing need not be concerned with protecting it. We should not forget his customary greeting: *"Pax et bonum."* Extending the Lord's peace may have been, by God's grace, what effected the peace that all too often eludes us.

PEACE BETWEEN CHRISTIANS

It is appropriate, then, for Francis to be seen as a sign of reconciliation for Roman Catholics and Lutherans. Francis is one medieval saint who has always been popular within the Protestant world. In the Apology of the Augsburg Confession, Philip Melancthon several times praised Francis as a "holy father" whose faith in God effected penance in life. Rembrandt, a Dutch Protestant, who usually chose biblical models, painted Francis at prayer. Francis calls us all back to the cross and to the power of God's reconciling love.

Eight hundred years after his birth, Roman Catholics and Lutherans meet to share Francis, exhuming him to probe his life, hoping that his powers of reconciliation still hover about his remains. There are ways Francis does not lead us. He does not call us to theological debate. In fact, we are disarmed by his refusal to use the weapons we prize. He was not a trained theologian or an ecclesiastical official. He instead sits among us in his rags, holding an open Bible on his lap, wishing us the peace of the Lord.

It is fortunate that when the movement toward reconciliation is gaining in popularity, the Church's liturgy has reinstituted the rite of the passing of the peace. Many worshipers understand this rite as a mere interlude, a chance for quick conversation, a break from liturgical action. As such the rite either works or fails, depending on the people involved. Are they comfortable with such interaction, or not? But the rite of peace has another level of meaning. After all, we do not exchange our own peace, a sort of morning hello now that we've finally awakened. It is the peace of the risen Lord Jesus which unites us even when we find ourselves apart. It is God's bond offered those who think they cannot bind themselves to one another. It is our prayer for God's grace among us. Thinking of the exchange of peace in this way will rid us of the anxiety about being friendly, all of a sudden, and will instead motivate us for that high liturgical act of being instruments of God's peace to one another. Thus also in our ecumenical dialogue—it is not our reservoirs of reconciliation which water the dry land. It is our baptism we share, God's water. It is God's gift of peace which makes our efforts toward peace effective. Francis can be a reminder for prayer, a sign of one who trusted in the reconciling power of God.

Francis can also be a reminder of the many things Lutherans and Roman Catholics already share. We share Christ on the cross, the Gospel message, the open Bible, the call to discipleship, the Eucharist, the good creation. The poor of the world have been given us to embrace. We have been given a Church which needs repair. The body of Christ is broken, we say; by that we mean not only the grace of Holy Communion, but also the necessity of the crucifixion and the fragmentation of the Church. No part of Christianity can or should believe that it has achieved the perfection of God's kingdom. Here is no talk about which church building needs less or more repair, St. Matthew Lutheran or St. Mary of the Angels Roman Catholic. Francis saw that the call was not to little things—wrecked chapels on Italian hillsides—but to the greatest of all: to dedicate oneself to the continuing life of the Church which is the body of Christ. That call comes to us all.

One of the main reasons why Francis was so effective as a reconciler was that he did not have to use his energies protecting vested interests. Perhaps this above all else hinders ecumenical dialogue—that we are always protecting ourselves, preserving our past, and shaping the world that will allow our future. Francis gave up this need for self-protection. He owned nothing and could be open to others. Thus, he becomes a symbol of openness to the world. We should determine how many of our traditions are gifts of life to the Church, budding branches for the ark, or how many are private vested interests which could safely be discarded. The story is told that when Francis' father hauled him before the bishop's court for selling company goods without authorization, Francis stripped himself naked, gave his clothes back to his father, and severed all his family bonds. In compassion, the bishop covered Francis' naked body with his own cope. What clothes from our past should we discard? What cope shelters us?

PEACE IN THE WORLD

As we move toward reconciliation within the Church, the world goes on its belligerent way. In our world, two fantasies are widespread: totalitarian inhumanity and idyllic perfection. The people of God should not be conned into believing that there is only a dread future in which hope is outmoded foolishness, or that humanity is on the way to absolute perfection. In assessing world progress, we should remember both the sin to which all humankind is subject and the grace of reconciliation which God offers us. In industrial nations there is a growing realization that neither fantasy will come to pass, because we will have long since annihilated ourselves.

It is not easy for any group of assembled Christians to agree on the wisest plan for preserving world peace. Some Christians feel that in a nuclear age strength is our only defense. They believe that talk of disarmament is idealistic and, in fact, reactionary. The major powers will refuse to be monitored, and smaller nations, too young to be veterans of compromise, will eventually acquire the bombs anyway. For these Christians, a well-locked door is the best deterrent to robbers. A bigger bomb is the most effective check against aggression.

Other Christians hope that some organization such as the United Nations will become a forum for international disputes. Whether we can insure our safety and control the decisions of every government is not the primary issue. These Christians think that the arms race is immoral. They feel that we cannot participate in such a race, because the very existence of such arms, far from being a deterrent to war, is rather assurance that nuclear bombs will eventually be employed.

What are our options, and how did we arrive at them? What influences shaped our attitudes toward peace and war? What history did we study? What wars have we experienced? What do we know about international politics? How has our ethic been formed? Surely when we can answer some of these questions our conversation with those with whom we disagree will be much more informed.

The Church has always had voices of pacifism within it. In the early centuries of the Church, the military was condemned because the ruling authority was pagan and emperor worship was obligatory for soldiers. Augustine made a distinction between just and unjust wars. Today no war can be considered "just" according to Augustine's standards, say some groups of

Christian pacifists. Granting the conditions of nuclear war, the harm done will inevitably be far greater than the political freedoms won. Thus, claim these Christians, all modern war is unjust and unjustifiable.

A significant organization urging this position is the Catholic Worker Movement, which began in 1933 as a Christian socialist response to the economic inequities apparent during the depression. Under the leadership of Dorothy Day, this movement became committed to Christian pacifism.

In Protestantism the "historic peace Churches" such as Mennonites and Quakers have given constant testimony to Christian pacifism. The Fellowship of Reconciliation is an interfaith pacifist organization with which the Lutheran Peace Fellowship is linked. Perhaps because of the nationalism associated with state churches in Europe and present even in North America, neither Lutheranism nor Roman Catholicism produced large numbers of pacifists. The Augsburg Confession, like traditional Catholic theology, retains Augustine's approval of just wars.

Some Christians claim a personal ethic of reconciliation but deny that the same ethic applies in the national and international arena. They believe that while I should not keep a gun to shoot a neighbor, a nation must keep many guns. Many Lutherans have such a belief based on the "two kingdoms" theory, which posits two simultaneous but separate reigns of God, one manifest in the Gospel and sacraments, the other hidden under the structures of the world. For these Christians, it is not contradictory for a peace-loving Christian to serve as a soldier.

Whether or not we can articulate it philosophically, many of us accept a kind of dualism, a division between the reign of God and the reign of evil. We live differently according to the realm in which we think we presently exist. The danger is that such dualistic behavior can become a cover for a lack of integrity. We need not be overly concerned with the world if we construe the ethic of Christ as a solely personal Word. We can ignore the call of the Church to be God's agents of reconciliation in the world. On the other hand, we can serve our country somewhat blindly, fighting for its rights to survive and thrive, as if God were undoubtedly on our side alone. After all, far from ordering the Roman soldiers to quit their jobs, Jesus told them to be content with their wages!

Ah, 'tis a muddle! There is no time like the anniversary of Francis to begin wading through it. We must inquire into the implications of our baptism for peacemaking in the world. Since the covenant with Abraham, God has promised to save the world through the chosen people. What is the content of such salvation? Is it salvation by God after the devastation of nuclear war? Is it life given by God because such destruction has been avoided? Is our biblical image the ark which alone survives the flood, or is it the midwife bringing God's creation to life?

It is a fine image, that horn, that ivory battle horn become a call to worship. So was Francis himself—first a knight in shining armor, last a ragged friar singing a song to soothe quarreling townspeople. Of course, we have to be willing to live without the armor. Reconciliation in Christ involves a baptismal robe, not a bulletproof vest. Righteousness, says Paul, is our breastplate. Surely, Francis would be delighted if we would use his horn and join him in his life of befriending: a call to war transformed into the call to worship, the weariness of battle become the joy of reconciliation.

We read Francis' call to prayer:[27]

> We Friars Minor, servants and worthless as we are, humbly beg and implore everyone to persevere in the true faith and in a life of penance; there is no other way to be saved. We beseech the whole world to do

this, all those who serve our Lord and God within the holy, catholic, and apostolic Church, together with the whole hierarchy, priests, deacons, subdeacons, acolytes, exorcists, lectors, porters, and all clerics and religious, male or female; we beg all children, big and small, the poor and the needy, kings and princes, laborers and farmers, servants and masters; we beg all virgins and all other women, married or unmarried; we beg all lay folk, men and women, infants and adolescents, young and old, the healthy and the sick, the little and the great, all peoples, tribes, families, and languages, all nations and all men everywhere, present and to come; we Friars Minor beg them all to persevere in the true faith and in a life of penance.

Rule of 1221

6
His Sign

One winter day St. Francis was coming to St. Mary of the Angels from Perugia with Brother Leo, and the bitter cold made them suffer keenly. St. Francis called to Brother Leo, who was walking a bit ahead of him, and he said, "Brother Leo, even if the Friars Minor in every country give a great example of holiness and integrity and good edification, nevertheless write down and note carefully that perfect joy is not in that."

And when he had walked on a bit, St. Francis called him again, saying: "Brother Leo, even if a Friar Minor gives sight to the blind, heals the paralyzed, drives out devils, gives hearing back to the deaf, makes the lame walk, and restores speech to the dumb, and, what is still more, brings back to life a man who has been dead four days, write that perfect joy is not in that."

And going on a bit, St. Francis cried out again in a strong voice: "Brother Leo, if a Friar Minor knew all languages and all sciences and Scripture, if he knew how to prophesy and to reveal not only the future but also the secrets of the consciences and minds of others, write down and note carefully that perfect joy is not in that."

And as they walked on, after a while St. Francis called again forcefully: "Brother Leo, Little Lamb of God, even if a Friar Minor could speak with the voice of an angel, and knew the courses of the stars and the powers of herbs, and knew all about the treasures of the earth, and if he knew the qualities of

birds and fishes, animals, humans, roots, trees, rocks, and wa-
ters, write down and note carefully that true joy is not in that."

And going on a bit farther, St. Francis called again strong-
ly: "Brother Leo, even if a Friar Minor could preach so well
that he should convert all infidels to the faith of Christ, write
that perfect joy is not there."

Now when he had been talking this way for a distance of
two miles, Brother Leo in great amazement asked him: "Father, I beg you in God's name to tell me where perfect joy is."

And St. Francis replied: "When we come to St. Mary of
the Angels, soaked by the rain and frozen by the cold, all soiled
with mud and suffering from hunger, and we ring at the gate
of the place and the brother porter comes and says angrily:
'Who are you?' And we say: 'We are two of your brothers.' And
he contradicts us, saying: 'You are not telling the truth. Rather
you are two rascals who go around deceiving people and steal-
ing what they give to the poor. Go away!' And he does not
open for us, but makes us stand outside in the snow and rain,
cold and hungry, until night falls—then if we endure all those
insults and cruel rebuffs patiently, without being troubled and
without complaining, and if we reflect humbly and charitably
that that porter really knows us and that God makes him speak
against us, oh, Brother Leo, write that perfect joy is there!

"And if we continue to knock, and the porter comes out in
anger, and drives us away with curses and hard blows like
bothersome scoundrels, saying: 'Get away from here, you dirty
thieves—go to the hospital! Who do you think you are? You
certainly won't eat or sleep here!'—and if we bear it patiently
and take the insults with joy and love in our hearts, oh, Brother
Leo, write that that is perfect joy!

"And if later, suffering intensely from hunger and the
painful cold, with night falling, we still knock and call, and crying loudly beg them to open for us and let us come in for the
love of God, and he grows still more angry and says: 'Those fel-

lows are bold and shameless ruffians. I'll give them what they deserve!' And he comes out with a knotty club, and grasping us by the cowl throws us onto the ground, rolling us in the mud and snow, and beats us with that club so much that he covers our bodies with wounds—if we endure all those evils and insults and blows with joy and patience, reflecting that we must accept and bear the sufferings of the Blessed Christ patiently for love of Him, oh, Brother Leo, write: that is perfect joy!

"And now hear the conclusion, Brother Leo. Above all the graces and gifts of the Holy Spirit which Christ gives to His friends is that of conquering oneself and willingly enduring sufferings, insults, humiliations, and hardships for the love of Christ. For we cannot glory in all those other marvelous gifts of God, as they are not ours but God's, as the Apostle says: 'What have you that you have not received?'

"But we can glory in the cross of tribulations and afflictions, because that is ours, and so the Apostle says: 'I will not glory save in the cross of our Lord Jesus Christ!' "

Little Flowers of St. Francis[28]

SERVANT OF THE CROSS

"We can glory in the cross," said Francis to Brother Leo. So Francis concluded his eloquent description of perfect joy. With the sign of the cross he summarized his inspiration for life, the sustenance of his vitality, the focus of his commitment.

Francis' subjection to the cross had begun long ago in the empty church of St. Damian when the lips of Christ, painted on that cross, spoke to him about his mission. Francis had seen a vision of the living Christ; he heard the cross and obeyed. When he taught his companions how to pray, he advised them to offer first the Lord's Prayer and then this prayer of the cross: "We adore you, Lord Jesus Christ, here and in all your

churches in the whole world, and we bless you, because by
your holy cross you have redeemed the world."[29] The story
tells that the Little Brothers reverenced every cross they
passed, whether a jeweled crucifix in a sanctuary or a rude
cross on a hillside. They should prostrate themselves, Francis
urged, in devotion to the cross of Christ. He himself meditated
on the cross, crying out over the love of God, mourning the
wounds of Christ. When asked the reason for his constant lament, he answered, "I must weep for the passion of my Lord
Jesus Christ; and I should not be ashamed to go weeping
through the whole world for his sake."[30] For Francis, devotion
to the cross was a sign of gratitude for Christ's passion.

Francis filled his letters with this sign of the cross. He reminded his readers about the passion; he reverenced the eucharistic bread as the body of Christ broken on the cross. He
imagined the depth of divine love which poured out blood in
death; he sought amendment of life as a response to the death
of Christ. One of his letters, still extant and enshrined as a relic
in Assisi, is signed both with Francis' own name, his signature,
and also with the "tau," the signature of the Christian. Where
Francis discovered the "tau" we do not know. Ezekiel first
mentions it as the sign on the forehead of God's elect. It is the
sacred mark of protection mentioned in the Book of Revelation, the sign of the cross which the Church traces on the forehead of the faithful at their baptism and of the penitent on Ash
Wednesday. This "T" mark, the "tau," merges with Francis
own name, because he took the sign of the cross as the sign for
himself.

THE STIGMATA OF CHRIST

Francis' devotion to Christ's cross occasioned the remarkable, mysterious experience which we call the stigmata. The
Franciscans had been given a mountain in the Apennines by a

friend of the Order. Francis used this desolate outcropping of rock as a place for religious retreat. He was praying alone there, fasting for forty days, in gratitude to St. Michael the Archangel. On September 14, 1224, the feast of the Holy Cross, Francis' companion called to him the opening lines of Morning Prayer. Francis did not return the expected response, and the Little Brother went to check on him. The brother found Francis, lying prostrate, still dazed by the vision of the Crucified which he had experienced.

The story tells that the vision was an Angel of the Lord, Christ as a seraph, the Crucified One in blinding light, his brilliant body held like a cross. The vision conveyed in terrifying splendor both the divine majesty and the human agony. In his religious ecstasy Francis experienced an identity with the Crucified which he later could not describe. He had so adored the Crucified One, he had so sought to imitate Christ, that he was marked with the cross of Christ and joined with Christ in praising God.

Francis spoke little about this experience in the few years remaining to him, but the sign of the cross was there. This was not only the "tau" sign cheerfully made, consciously drawn, as part of Francis' signature. Now he had other marks, deeper signs—the stigmata. After the experience of religious ecstasy, it became known that Francis' body bore the five wounds of Christ. Bonaventure writes:

> His hands and feet appeared pierced through the center with nails, the heads of which were in the palms of his hands and on the instep of each foot, while the points stuck out on the opposite side. The heads were black and round, but the points were long and bent back, as if they had been struck by a hammer; they rose above the surrounding flesh and stood out from it. His right side seemed as if it had been pierced with

a lance and was marked with a livid scar which often
bled, so that his habit and trousers were stained.[31]

Although Francis attempted to hide these bloody signs of his
life with Christ, his closest companions caught sight of the
wounds under wrap. The brothers who laundered his habit
used cold water to remove the blood stains. Thomas of Celano
writes that "true love for Christ has transformed this lover into
the very image of Christ."[32] Not a beatific light emanating
from his face, not the power of miracles, not a royal crown, but
a bloody habit and wounded hands were his image of Christ.
He wore his sleeves longer now, and put socks on his bare feet,
as if these wounds were private, inexplicable signs of a visit
from the Crucified.

Two years later, Francis died. Those who attended his
body after his death were amazed by the wounds still present,
still red with blood against the stark whiteness of the dead skin.
On his body he bore the marks of Christ, they said, quoting
Paul. They revered this simple singer of ballads, this disinherit-
ed bum, this itinerant preacher, as one uniquely associated
with the suffering Christ.

One story goes further, recalling that at his death a flock of
skylarks who gathered to praise or to mourn flew off to heaven
in the shape of a cross, remembering in their reverence that
sign which was both the impetus to Francis' vibrant vocation
and the stigmata on his wracked and bleeding body.

THE WAY OF THE CROSS

Francis' sign was the cross. The Crucified One was both
the model and the source of his life. To be like Christ, Francis
embraced Lady Poverty. To follow the Christ proclaimed in
the Gospel, Francis heard and preached the Word. He was devoted to the Eucharist because he adored the Crucified One.

He repaired churches because they were houses for the worship of Christ. He united with all creation to praise God because in Christ he saw the incarnation of God in all the created world. He effected reconciliation because as the companion of Christ he extended God's peace to all. He heard the Crucified speak because he identified with the sufferings of Christ. "In all things Christ," one could say of Francis.

Both his own Franciscan Order and Roman Catholicism in general have been nourished by Francis' vision of the Crucified One. Franciscan devotion to the cross led to the development of a pious exercise called the Way of the Cross. While stations of the cross were erected for devotional purposes in various places during the first Christian millennium, the practice blossomed especially when the Franciscans took charge of the holy places in Jerusalem following the crusades of the fourteenth century. Respect for the sites along the route of the crucifixion led to the practice of setting up models of the road to Calvary in parish yards and on monastery grounds. Usually there are fourteen stations, marked with shrines. The pious penitent travels the Via Dolorosa from the condemnation of Christ by Pilate to the burial of Jesus in the tomb. The faithful walk from one station to another, meditating on the passion of Christ, praying for amendment of life and for the coming of God's kingdom. Originally only Franciscan churches could possess stations of the cross. Today, virtually every Roman Catholic church in the world has on its walls or in its floors some representation of the way of the cross.

These devotions to the cross and other such religious exercises have lately fallen from favor. Excesses of sentimentality—to say nothing of maudlin art—are embarrassing to the contemporary mind. Still, we might grieve at the passing of such piety which at its best was a devotion to the cross of Christ and an inspiration to imitation of his life. These practices tended to offer the image of the cross as the essence of Christ. While it is true that one image is not the total entity, we are bereft if we deprive ourselves completely of such images. Recent emphasis on the communal nature of Christian worship has further demoted devotional practices which tend to be highly individualistic. Nonetheless, these devotions were one way that Francis' vision of the cross was kept alive among us. Francis was overwhelmed by the cross, his life altered by a crucifix, his body wounded by its nails. Such intense Christian experience should find ways to be sustained among us as well.

Since the death of Francis, more than three hundred people are said to have had an experience of the stigmata. Some have had actual wounds like those of Francis. Others have experienced excruciating pains in palms, feet and side. In some cases the stigmata appear and disappear; in others the manifestation is constant. How do such wounds and pains come to be? Are they self-inflicted? Are they real physical lesions given miraculously by God? Are they always the result of an ecstatic vision? What is the connection between these visions, physical debility and emotional imbalance? Does it matter? What about evidence that the nails of a crucified victim were usually hammered through the wrist, not the palms? Our penchant for scientific explanations for every phenomenon is confronted by the testimony of many who saw such wounds on Francis, and who explained them as a precious gift from God, testifying that likeness to Christ is the goal of every baptized Christian.

Reaching consensus about the origin of such phenomena is not the point. Christianity and, indeed, all world religions try to interpret the events of the world, natural and otherwise, in the truth of God. Christians see events in the light of Christ. The point of Francis' stigmata and of other similar experiences is incorporation into Christ, imitation of Christ as religious devotion, likeness to Christ as the worship of God. We may or may not wish to experience such religious ecstasy, but we should stand respectfully before those who have. We also seek in some way to be graced with a vision of God.

THEOLOGY OF THE CROSS

Lutherans are as devoted to the cross in their own way as Francis was in his. The television preacher Robert Schuller recently told some Lutheran seminarians that they talk too much about the cross. Indeed, "the theology of the cross" is a shorthand expression often used to characterize Lutheran theology. Martin Luther's vision of God was expressed verbally, intellectually, while Francis' was expressed dramatically, emotionally. Luther was a university theologian, not an itinerant troubadour, but Luther's vision of God was, like that of Francis, a vision of the cross. Jurgen Moltmann, a contemporary theologian, speaks of the "crucified God," using the same radical language which we know in Luther. "Apart from this man there is no God," wrote Luther regarding the humanity of God in the Crucified One. The Lutheran gift is to see the paradoxes present in Christianity, the throne of God as the cross on Calvary, the divine splendor as the crown of thorns, the light of God as the darkness of Good Friday. Lutherans take all religious language—God, splendor, life, goodness, holiness—and subject it to the cross, to the Crucified One and his death. When Luther interpreted all Scriptures through Christ, he found not some glorified demigod but a crucified man enlivening the words of Old and New Testaments alike.

Faithful devotion to the cross of Christ and to its reality in human life hindered Luther from closer association with some of the other Protestant Reformers. In characteristically blunt tones, Luther one day shouted in exaggeration, "I'd rather drink blood with the Pope than wine with the Swiss!" He meant that the sign of the cross still was revered as alive and salutary among both Roman Catholics and Lutherans of the sixteenth century. Our mutual devotion to the cross, whether expressed dramatically and emotionally or intellectually and theologically, remains one of the great bonds between Lutherans and Roman Catholics.

Lutherans are not devoid of devotional piety either. It is common for Lutherans to hold Lenten services in which the sign of the cross is exalted in hymns about the passion and portrayed artistically. Homilies about the passion figure prominently, making Lent a kind of communal way of the cross. A not uncommon name for Lutheran parishes is "Holy Cross." It is a custom to begin the school year in Lutheran parochial schools with an observance of the feast of the Holy Cross and its lessons of paradox. In the Lutheran hymnal, the famous Christmas carol "What Child Is This?" retains the original juxtaposition of the manger with the line, "Nails, spear, shall pierce him through/The cross be borne for me, for you." That's very Lutheran—to recall the crucifixion and death of Jesus on Christmas, the celebration of his birth.

THE RECONCILING CROSS

We contemporary Lutherans and Roman Catholics stand together under the cross, like John and Mary, one writing paradoxical theology, the other adoring the body of Christ. The joy is that we stand there together, John and Mary, at the cross, our joy coming from the cross, our perfect joy in that cross. We live at a time when, standing there together, we are beginning to recognize one another, to call one another by name, to reverence one another, to respect one another's gifts. As joy is in Christ, so is reconciliation, not in official dialogues or in living room conversations. As the cross of Christ is reconciliation of the world to God, so is the cross our reconciliation with one another. The inspiration of Francis, the intercession of Francis,

our discussions about Francis—these will not effect our reconciliation. Rather, that cross which gave Francis his inexplicable
wounds and his greatest joy will achieve it.

The cross is one and the same for us. The cross signed at
our baptism is one cross for all Christians. The cross preached
in our sermons, the cross with which we are blessed each
week, the cross with which our foreheads are marked, the
cross which finally stands over our casket—this is one and the
same cross for all of us. In a world increasingly pagan, the cross
is sheer nonsense. Read Friedrich Nietzsche at the close of the
last century leading our age in ribald mockery of the God of
the cross. The differences between us seem increasingly unim-
portant compared with the overwhelming vision we share—
seen in different guises, described in different ways, lived
through different pieties—the vision of the Crucified One.

Francis' vision of the crucified one speaking at St. Damian
shaped his life into holiness. His stigmatization began two
years of ever intensifying mystical ecstasy. He drew away
more and more from the world, closer and closer to God. The
Christian is convinced that the way to God, the only effective
path to heaven, is through the cross. The cross is the very sign
of God on earth. We say with the emperor Constantine, "In
this sign we shall conquer." In the thirteenth century, Franciscans began painting depictions of the cross as a bountiful tree,
the fruit on the branches the saintly virtues. The cross is also
our sign of the tree of life. That archetypal religious symbol of
the great world tree, we Christians have found to be living still
on Calvary. Together with Francis, we say, "By your cross you
have redeemed the world."

We pray Francis' Praises of God:[33]

> You are holy, Lord, the only God,
>   And your deeds are wonderful.

You are strong.
>
>You are great.
>
>You are the Most High,
>
>You are almighty.
>
>You, holy Father, are
>
>King of heaven and earth.

You are Three and One,
>
>Lord God, all good.
>
>You are Good, all Good, supreme Good,
>
>Lord God, living and true.

You are love,
>
>You are wisdom,
>
>You are humility,
>
>You are endurance.
>
>You are rest,
>
>You are peace.
>
>You are joy and gladness.
>
>You are justice and moderation.
>
>You are all our riches,
>
>And you suffice for us.

You are beauty,
>
>You are gentleness.
>
>You are our protector,
>
>You are our guardian and defender.
>
>You are courage.
>
>You are our haven and our hope.

You are our faith,
>
>Our great consolation.
>
>You are our eternal life,
>
>Great and wonderful Lord,
>
>God almighty,
>
>Merciful Savior.

We close with Francis' blessing to Brother Leo, signed with the tau:

God bless you and keep you.
     May God smile on you, and be merciful to you;
May God turn his regard toward you
     and give you peace.
May God bless you, Brother Leo.
          T

Notes

1. Francis, *Praises before the Office;* Omnibus, p. 139.
1a. *Legend of the Three Companions* 7; Omnibus 896–97.
2. Bonaventure, *Major Life,* 6; Omnibus 684.
3. Francis, *Rule of 1221,* 4 and 5; Omnibus, 60–61.
4. Francis, *Testament;* Omnibus, 67.
5. Thomas of Celano, *Second Life,* 6; Omnibus, 366.
6. Luther, *Magnificat;* Luther's Works, Vol. 21, p. 299.
7. Luther, *Magnificat;* Luther's Works, Vol. 21, p. 301.
8. Francis, *Rule of 1221;* Omnibus, 31.
9. Francis, *Praises of the Virtues;* Omnibus, 132–34.
10. Thomas of Celano, *First Life,* 22–23; Omnibus, 246–47.
11. *Little Flowers* 30; Omnibus, 1376.
12. Francis, *Rule of 1221,* 1; Omnibus, 31–32.
13. Thomas of Celano, *First Life,* 86; Omnibus, 301.
14. Francis, *Fifth Office;* Omnibus, 154–55.
15. Thomas of Celano, *Second Life,* 10, 11; Omnibus, 370–71.
16. Bonaventure, *Major Life,* 3, 10; Omnibus, 652.
17. Francis, *Testament;* Omnibus, 67.
18. Francis, *Letter to General Chapter,* 1; Omnibus, 104.
19. Francis, *Letter to General Chapter;* Omnibus, 108.
20. *Little Flowers,* 21; Omnibus, 1348–50.
21. Thomas of Celano, *Second Life,* 166; Omnibus, 497.
22. Thomas of Celano, *Miracles,* 32; Omnibus, 548.
23. Bonaventure, *Major Life,* 8, 1; Omnibus, 688.
24. Francis, *Canticle of Brother Sun;* Omnibus, 130–31.

25. *Legend of Perugia* 44; Omnibus, 1022–24.
26. Thomas of Celano, *First Life*, 23; Omnibus, 248.
27. Francis, *Rule of 1221*, 23; Omnibus, 51.
28. *Little Flowers*, 8; Omnibus, 1318–1320.
29. Francis, *Testament;* Omnibus, 67.
30. *Legend of the Three Companions*, 14; Omnibus 901.
31. Bonaventure, *Major Life*, 13, 3; Omnibus, 731.
32. Thomas of Celano, *Second Life*, 135; Omnibus, 472.
33. Francis, *Praises of God and Blessing for Brother Leo;* Omnibus 124–25.

All citations of the *Omnibus* are taken from *St. Francis of Assisi—Writings and Early Biographies: English Omnibus of the Sources for the Life of St. Francis,* edited by Marion A. Habig, Third Revised Edition (Franciscan Herald Press, 1973), and are quoted by permission of the publishers.

Program Suggestions

These suggestions for cooperative projects and activities between Lutheran and Roman Catholic parishes are arranged according to the chapter topics of this book.

1 HIS LADYLOVE (Francis, Knight of Poverty)

1. Organize a joint service of the *Transitus* of St. Francis on the evening of October 3 (this is a Sunday evening in 1982). After the service, participants can anticipate the Poverello's feast day (October 4) by "feasting" together on salad, bread and water. The money saved on food should be collected from each participant and given to the poor directly or through an agency of either Church.
2. Invite speakers to a discussion of the worldwide ministries in which each Church is engaged on behalf of the poor in third world countries, such as Lutheran World Relief and Catholic Relief Services. Adopt a parish or mission in one of those countries for a year by making a definite financial and spiritual commitment.
3. Organize high schoolers and young adults in a project of investigation and remedial help in the local area where poor people can be found. Find out the facts and then do something concrete for poor people. Let them do something for you.
4. Begin a Christmas crèche project—research, plan, build. Let Lutherans build one for Roman Catholics and vice

versa. Have a presentation program at the beginning of Advent.

5. Plan and create banners with themes of poverty, justice and peace for one another's churches. Organize a presentation ceremony.

2   HIS CALL (Francis, Herald of the Gospel)

1. Have a pulpit exchange on one Sunday in October (or during Week of Prayer for Christian Unity).

2. Organize joint Bible study groups on such topics as poverty, vocation, discipleship, justice, peace, penance/repentance, reconciliation.

3. Help the pastors to prepare their Sunday sermons by participating in a joint weekday discussion group which studies, meditates upon and shares thoughts about the scriptural readings for the following Sunday or Sundays.

4. Organize a joint study group to discuss the relationship between the Service of the Word and the Service of the Table (Eucharist). Study one another's worship rites. Discuss one another's eucharistic practices.

5. Review the various Lutheran/Roman Catholic dialogues, national and international, and discover how the dialogues employ Scripture. Discuss how the results of these dialogues can and should affect preaching. (Cf. Chapter 6 of *Exploring the Faith We Share,* ed. by Stone and LaFontaine, Paulist Press, 1980).

3   HIS WORK (Francis, Renewer of the Church)

1. Visit one another's churches for the main service on a Sunday in October (or another convenient time). Exchange choirs, or bring them both together for a joint choral recital.

2. Organize discussion groups on *Exploring the Faith We*

Share (Paulist Press, 1980) and *Francis: A Saint We Share* (Paulist, 1982).

3. Prepare and share in a joint service of praise (Morning and/or Evening Prayer) on a Sunday in October (or other convenient time). Hold a social hour afterward.

4. Organize a retreat for high schoolers and young adults on the theme of "vocation." Ask representatives from the various ministries of each Church as well as from the various stations in life to speak or lead discussions.

5. Invite "experts" to speak at a clergy conference on the theme of Christian discipleship. Invite the same speaker(s) to present the sermon/homily at both churches on a Sunday in October (or other convenient time).

4   HIS FRIENDS (Francis, Brother of Nature)

1. Prepare a service of the Word at which there will be a blessing of pets and domestic animals. Let children from both churches share the major parts.

2. Research, plan and present lesson plans on Francis and his ideas and attitudes toward creation for primary and secondary school levels.

3. Organize neighborhood conservation projects. Offer ecology awards to the best and most successful projects.

4. View the film, "Brother Sun, Sister Moon." Organize discussions on Francis as "patron saint of ecology and ecologists."

5. Research, plan and present a program or display on "St. Francis in Art" or "St. Francis and the Arts," using film, ceramics, photography, sculpture, paintings.

6. Construct a large *papier-mâché* wolf for sanctuary use. On it pin cards bearing parishioners' expressions of fears, anxieties, sins, alienations. Hold a service in which the "wolf is tamed" by the word of God in Scripture.

5   HIS BEFRIENDING (Francis, Peacemaker for God)

1. Form discussion groups on the theme of peacemaking and peacemakers. Discover concrete opportunities for peacemaking in self, family, neighborhood, parish.
2. Organize a joint liturgical service of penance/repentance and reconciliation, using the ritual of one or the other Church.
3. View the filmstrip "Together in Hope: Lutherans and Roman Catholics in Dialogue" (Franciscan Communications Center, Lutheran Film Associates). Organize discussion groups based on the filmstrip.
4. Organize a neighborhood clean-up, fix-up project. Do the same for one another's church facilities.
5. Organize a dinner and discussion for the two parish councils and the clergy of both churches.

6   HIS SIGN (Francis, Servant of the Cross)

1. Research, prepare and participate in a joint service of the "Stations of the Cross," using chorales, film, photography, art, ceramics.
2. Dramatize the life of Francis as "Lover of Jesus Crucified," by preparing and presenting "playlets" written and acted by primary and/or secondary church-school students.
3. Organize a joint discussion group to consider Christian asceticism and spirituality today. Begin plans to celebrate Lent and Good Friday together in some or several ways next year.
4. See project 4.6. above.
5. Adapt the programs suggested under all of the above categories to your own needs, energies, circumstances, resources, and facilities. Reject all or some of the above in preference to your own ideas.

RESOURCES

1. *Francis,* NFCC, Graymoor, Garrison, NY 10524. This is the official newsletter of the St. Francis of Assisi Eighth Centenary, published by National Franciscan Communications Conference.

2. Franciscan Communications Center, 1229 South Sante St., Los Angeles, CA 90015. Filmstrips: "Together in Hope," "Toward a Human World Order," "The Gift of Land." Films: "The First Christmas Crib," "Behold This Child: The Christmas Stories of Matthew and Luke."

3. St. Anthony Messenger Press, 1615 Republic St., Cincinnati, OH 45210. Pamphlet: "Christian Unity: Our Unfinished Task," by Thaddeus Horgan, S.A. Special issue of "Catholic Update." Ask for catalogue of Franciscan Resources.

4. Charisma Press. St. Francis Seminary, 459 River Rd., PO Box 263, Andover, MA 01810. Book: "In the Womb of the Cave: Journal of Writings of Francis of Assisi."

5. *Today's Catholic Teacher* (Vol. 15, No. 1, Sept. 1981). Lesson plans: "Peace and All Good."

6. *Franciscans at Prayer* (English-Speaking Conference of the Order of Friars Minor, 232 S. Home Ave., Pittsburgh, PA 15202). Prayer Book.

7. "Francis of Assisi: The Last Christian," book by A. Holl (Doubleday and Co., 245 Park Ave., New York, NY 10017).

8. "St. Francis and the Song of Brotherhood," book by Eric Doyle (Seabury Press, Seabury Service Center, Somers, CT 06071).

9. "Francis of Assisi," book by Arnaldo Fortini (Crossroad Publishing Co., 18 E. 41st St., New York, NY 10017).

10. "Brother Sun, Sister Moon," film (Paramount Pictures, 5451 Marathon St., Hollywood, CA 90038. Phone: (213) 462-0700 or (800) 421-4432).

11. "Francis: Brother of the Universe," comic book, 50 pages with study-discussion guides (Paulist Press, 545 Island Rd., Ramsey, NJ 07446).

12. *St. Francis of Assisi,* book by Lawrence Cunningham with photographs by Dennis Stock (Harper & Row, 1700 Montgomery St., San Francisco, CA 94111).